SPIRIT
DRIVEN
SUCCESS

By Dani Johnson

SPECIAL
FREE CD OFFER!!!

Get Dani Johnson's *"Conquering the Financial Kingdom"* CD FREE!
Just visit **www.DaniJohnson.com/freecfkcd**

We'll also give you a complimentary membership to our
members only site where you'll get access to exclusive
Dani Johnson audio and video content to help you
experience more Spirit Driven Success in your life!

Go ahead, do it now!
www.DaniJohnson.com/freecfkcd

DEDICATIONS

*Father in Heaven in the name of Jesus have
Your way with this book.*

*To Kristina, Arika, Cabe, Roman and Micah.
May you never limit the limitless God.
Set the world on fire with your passion for Him.*

ACKNOWLEDGEMENTS

Wow! This is crazy to be writing this right now. First, thank you Jesus Christ for saving my soul—for being my Strong Tower. Truly, I AM NOTHING WITHOUT YOU! Thank you for allowing me to do this and for bringing the hands to help. All Glory is Yours.

To the most amazing husband on the planet—Hans! You have powerfully used your gifts to push our message out into the marketplace. I love you more than words can say.

To all five of my babies—you support me and believe in OUR calling. You are the best a mom could ever ask for. If you weren't who you are I couldn't do what I do. I love you sooo much!

Marla Fairfield—Girl you so attacked this project and pressed through obstacles to bring it to pass. The hoops you jumped through were insane. Thanks for doing whatever it took to get this done.

Holly McClure you showed up out of nowhere and shocked us with the precious gift of making this happen. Thanks for the all-nighters by the fire. Thanks for pressing through while others said it was impossible to get done. Ha! Here it is.

Jack and Lavonne for allowing God to use you to save our marriage years ago. If Hans and I weren't together this would not be happening. Your wise counsel is priceless and you taught me how to stand on the true Word of God. Thank you for your unconditional love, belief, encouragement and support.

Ruth Brown for teaching me how to fight in the spirit realm and to not back down, and teaching me how to pray. For loving me unconditionally through a lot of my immaturity through the years. I am forever grateful to you.

JP—Dude... look at this! Thank you so much for seeing something in a 19-year-old kid that she couldn't see herself. Thanks for always believing in me even when I didn't believe in myself.

Ed Negrelli—Thank you for planting the first seed in me when I was young and stupid, unbelieving, untrained, and ignorant. You were the first one to get me to think bigger than me. Look how God used you to touch one life who has touched hundreds of thousands of lives. I am forever grateful for you.

Mona McGrady for being our advocate and for the 2AM—4AM night watch. Your years of dedication to the vision. Can you believe God lets us do this? Nuts!

Jeribai Tascoe, you have done a phenomenal job on everything you touch. Your gift in design is outrageous. You have been a huge blessing to our team.

Our team of intercessors… look what God has done! Your prayers are fruitful. Thank you for your years of service and your commitment to the call.

The entire DJC team—Brian, Marla, Gerri, Mona, Joseph, Jenn, Tim, JP, Ed, Jeribai, Isa, Ryan, Nina, LauraLee, Andrew, Arika, Diana, Judi, Robyn, Elyssa, Tammy, Jordan, Gabe, Jeremy, Patrick, Laurie, Kim, Penny, and Juana. Wow!

I could write another book on you alone! Thank you for your dedication, commitment, persistence, and tenacity. Thank you for applying what you have learned and reaching higher. Thank you for all the hands that have touched this project in one way or another. Thank you for your love for Him.

Our clients—You are our friends; you are amazing! Thank you for running with this teaching, embracing it and attacking the marketplace with it. You have produced results that have caught the attention of nations. This adventure would be useless to me without you.

Mom, thank you for not aborting me. Look what God has done. I love you.

What others have said about
Spirit Driven Success

"Until I listened to your training, I thought I was going to have to choose between having a spiritual life and having a business. Hearing how you have been able to balance between the two has given me hope."

~ Fran W.

"The training was authentic, energizing, and multi-disciplined. This was the absolute best use of my time and money!"

~ Pamela B.

"My husband and I are new in business. The Lord is showing us the awesome truth of the need for the church to honor the "kings of the marketplace". We are different now for God's glory because of Dani's obedience to use her gifting to set the captives free. Thank you Dani for being that weapon in God's mighty hand to set me free!"

~ Sonya C.

"At the Spiritual Equipping Service I opened my heart to what you had to say and I received great words of wisdom that I can apply to my life and my business. Thank you for taking the time and effort to share your heart and faith with us."

~ Craig U.

"The Spirit Driven Success CD series is my all-time favorite! It's so great to be able to implement spiritual values and principles not only into my life, but also my business. There is a simple map of success for all areas of life, family and business and Dani shares this plan that helps to create balance, a sense of peace and faith and gets you to take Action towards the person God intended you to be."

~ Kimber K.

"Dani Johnson's Spirit Driven Success™ training has shattered all the walls that confined me to striving for more and pleasing everyone else at the cost of my own freedom. I have my life back now. Dani has taught me to hear God's voice and follow His direction by helping me understand what His word says about life, love, business, parenting, everything! Her practical and honest style has taught me victory through Jesus in every area of my life. If you want more confidence and direction in your life, don't wait another minute, start today."

~ Tracy S.

"Thank you for the Spiritual Equipping Session. What Christ has done through you has changed our lives forever. I'll never look at business or relationships the same way again!"

~ Angela F.

"Through your training, my husband Mark and I both learned that we worshipped an idol called FEAR... and because of that a famine was produced in our lives. The word of God jumped out of your mouth into our hearts and God revealed to us why we have not moved forward."

~ Laura M.

"I have heard the Lord speak to my heart in many ways and in so many areas, I have been making the wrongs, right. My spiritual life with God has changed and He has been changing me daily. I would rather have Jesus more than anything else. I know the rest will come. I could have all the money in the world, but if things weren't right with Jesus, it would all be in vain!"

~ Crystal P.

"Thank you so much for all that you do to minister life and healing in the area of personal development and wealth to hundreds of thousands, if not millions of people around the world. One of the things I admire most about you is the fact that you give glory and honor to God the Father and the Lord Jesus Christ in everything that you do. I was thrilled and exhilarated when I attended First Steps Spiritual Equipping and had the freedom to worship and praise Him. As a believer, I feel safe submitting myself to your training and referring my friends, family and associates to you as well."

~ Jennifer R.

"The Lord inspired me in your message. My business has exploded!"

~ Chris W.

"My life is on FIRE! Not only has your program ignited my business, but it has affected every area of my life! Communicating with others has always been easy for me, yet after your training, I find myself interfacing with others in a completely different way. What a gift!

~ Cynthia K.

"The power of working with integrity and excellence, this is what I have been looking for! I knew there had to be a better way, where people were honored and not abused. You showed us how. Thank you for following your call."

~ Kai Druhl.

"I can implement this 'stuff' with my family, my 7 kids, and my husband!"

~ Tami G.

"Dani's training taught us how to become professionals. Get to First Steps to Success; it will change your business, it will change your life!"

~ Joe T.

"I praise God for you!! Not only am I learning business strategies, but also my entire life is changing, and everyone around me notices!! I love you!"

~ Michelle A.

"You are truly blessed and anointed by God! Some of this info isn't a 'new word', but it's a 'now word' that's very relevant and needed. Your teachings have turned my life around. Continued blessings to you!!!"

~ Becky J.

"Dani, this is what I've been missing and looking for! God bless!"

~ Michael C.

"You have amazing tips that are simple and doable. As an art teacher of 800 young children from first through 8th grade, whom I teach week after week, I thought I knew how to teach until I saw you teach! Now I am using your teaching techniques in the classroom, and they work!"

~ Stella D.

"I'm so blessed that God brought me to you! I was listening for a change! I got FINANCIAL FREEDOM!!!"

~ Karen U.

"Prior to coming to Dani, I was a recently divorced workaholic who didn't value God, myself or other people. After plugging into First Steps to Success and Dani Johnson, I paid off over $12,000 in debt in 6 months. On top of that, I remarried my ex-husband, I'm having more fun than I've ever had in my life, and my confidence is at an all time high!"

-Kristin H.

"Thank you for your faith-based program that has not only impacted my business, but my life as well."

~ Becky W.

"Thank you again for reminding me that I need to keep it simple. Thank you also for reminding me that it doesn't matter how long it takes me to get there, just to get there."

~ Lesia C.

"Prior to Dani's training, I spent so much time working, and didn't' want to hear anything my husband had to say to me because

I thought that I was the "bread winner" of the house. I thought I was coming to Dani to learn how to grow my business, but I had a new revelation. I realized God had chosen my husband for me and that he was the King in my life and I had to lift him up. I learned how to balance my life and within days, my whole life started to change."

~ LaShonda C.

"I was a doubter, but now I have no other choice but to believe and lead others! Dani and her 'folks' live what they teach!"

~ Thomas A.

"I achieved a six-figure income, but I was absolutely miserable. I had no time or freedom, didn't see my children and was losing control of my life. After coming to Dani Johnson, I've learned so many skills to gain manageability of my own life and business. It's improved my marriage. I now earn a multiple six-figure income – paid off over $100,000 worth of debt. I haven't seen one person who hasn't been phenomenally affected by the training, equipping, and the personal growth that occurs with Dani Johnson."

~ Renae H.

"Being able to plug into Spirit Driven Success, I've learned so many things that have set me free. It's allowed me to raise my children for success instead of bondage. It's allowed me to completely restore and heal my marriage. This is something that will completely equip you and teach you to open up your heart and allow him to work in your life and to start living in peace instead of constant resistance."

~ Anonymous

FORWARD

"You are the light of the world. A city on a hill cannot be hidden... let your light shine before men, that they may see your good deeds and praise your Father in heaven."

Matthew 5:14, 16

S THERE MORE to success than driving fancy cars, living in a big house, dropping important names at cocktail parties or taking exotic vacations? Is there more to life than volunteering for yet another church program while you struggle to pay your bills and make ends meet?

Are we really being told the complete truth about what success is and what success is not, from our society, the media and our churches? Does the church's traditional definition of success stand against God's biblical definition of success? Is it really possible to achieve your dreams, yet still do the work of your Father in Heaven?

In *Spirit Driven Success*, Dani Johnson answers all of these questions and more. However, she doesn't stop there. Dani shows you specific changes that you need to make in your life right now, in order to start experiencing immediate results in every area of your life.

Spirit Driven Success offers a radical new approach to examining something as old as time. It is a message that is long overdue and has already changed countless lives who have attended Dani's live seminars and events.

As a successful business woman, mega-entrepreneur, mother of 5 and loving wife, Dani is the real deal, through and through. She lives and breathes what she teaches. I know this because as both her husband and lifelong business partner, I've personally witnessed her heart and character behind the scenes, in our business, personal and family life. I can tell you that her integrity, sincerity and desire to equip others to succeed is surpassed only by her passion to serve God.

In *Spirit Driven Success*, Dani will share in her raw candid, straight from the gut style, the biblical success secrets she has discovered and applied in her own life - from homeless to millions she has become one of the most sought after business coaches in the world today.

The concepts in *Spirit Driven Success* have shown tens of thousands of others how to improve their lives spiritually, mentally, emotionally, physically and financially. Will you be next?

What's the reason you have this book in your hands right now? Are you looking for change? Are you looking for financial independence? Do you want to take your career or business to new levels of growth, prosperity and success? Do you want to create a legacy for your family that lasts generations?

This book will show you HOW to do it, so that your Father in Heaven may be glorified.

~ Hans Johnson

TABLE OF CONTENTS

INTRODUCTION

I GREW UP IN a home filled with daily verbal and physical abuse, from a drug-addicted father, pathetically enabled by my indifferent, drug addicted mother. My two sisters and I were often the targets of my father's violent temper in a home where constant emotional turmoil, verbal assaults, physical beatings, and even sexual abuse, were daily events throughout my childhood and teenage years.

While still in my teens, I escaped my psychotic home life and began working a number of short-term jobs, never really excelling at anything. Whatever I attempted to do, a day didn't go by that I didn't hear the constant barrage of my father's criticism ringing in my ears, "You're fat, you're ugly, and good for nothing!"

In my search to prove him wrong, and prove to myself that I could break-free from the bondage of his cursed words, I made a decision to become an entrepreneur. Within a few months and with only the education of hard knocks, I failed miserably. I realized I needed knowledge, skills, and intensive training, to equip my determination. Although I could not afford it at the time, I made a decision to invest in some business training classes. It was the best money I ever spent and for the first time in my life, I invested in me!

Within six months I became one of the top sales leaders in my company, enjoying all of the income and praise that comes with being a young, top producer. I likewise gained the confidence I needed to succeed in a highly competitive business world. I was treated like a celebrity, had plenty of money, and people were actually seeking me out, to see what they could learn from me. From me! The "fat, ugly, and good for nothing" entrepreneur, was on a mission to prove that the negative words her father spoke over her, were wrong.

While at a training event, one of the attendees came over and asked me if he could "pick my brain" for some business tips. He was movie star handsome, incredibly charming, and he made me feel wanted, appreciated, and important. We fell head-over-heels in love, spent a romantic and passionate week together, and married in a romantic whirlwind. I was convinced I had finally found my, "Happily Ever After", perfect life.

Within four months, my handsome husband left me for another woman, took all of my money, left me with a $35,000 debt and exactly $2.03 to my name. At that same time, my business was embezzled by a man who had actually taught me a few things about building my business. I was devastated, abandoned, confused, alone and very scared.

Everything I owned was packed into my tiny car. I lived at public beaches, slept in my car, showered in public facilities, and tried to sort through the devastation I felt over losing everything: my husband, business, savings, friends, my dignity, but worst of all, my dreams. I lost all hope and had no vision and no future. I had become the awful words my father spoke over me.

I managed to get a job as a cocktail waitress spending most of my days smoking pot with friends and working afternoon shifts. It was Christmas time and at a work party, I did something I swore I would never do, I was offered a line of cocaine and I took it! The next day I found myself on a beach, desperate for another line of cocaine, anything to numb the pain of my existence and make me forget my horrendous life.

While people were partying on the beach, I got up and walked into the ocean. As I waded out to the waves, I dove under one that was about to break and when I stood up, I heard the words: "Pick up your mat and walk". I instantly went to my beach towel, picked it up and left. As I drove down the highway, I realized a change had come over me. The drugged and foggy feeling was gone and the craving for cocaine was gone. Moments before I was gripped by an overpowering urge to get more drugs but now, that desperation was completely GONE. Gone were the angry thoughts, the depression, the despair, the hopelessness.

I did not question the voice because I knew it was God. And I heard the words, "God did not intend for you to be mediocre and average, this life you're living is not for you."

The next day I started a business from the trunk of my car and a pay phone booth. I was completely focused; no more whining, crying the blues, complaining, and no more pity parties. Within a couple of days, I made $2000.00 and within my first year of business, I made a quarter of a million dollars. By the second year, I made my first million. All by the age of 23! Since then I have made millions and millions of dollars building businesses and helping other people to succeed financially as well.

I have had outrageous success as well as devastating hardships - life is not perfect just because you believe in God. With every step, God has been in every circumstance of my life. I am blown away by His incredible love. I marvel at each experience God has both blessed me with and brought me through. Each experience has made me who I am today.

God's love is, and has always been, constant. How precious and forgiving is the God I turned my back on years ago. Even through my hurt, rejection, and anger at life, He was the Father I never had, who loved me, disciplined me, and welcomed home His prodigal daughter.

My life is much more than I ever dreamed possible. Blessed with a loving husband, five wonderful children, an amazing circle of friends and an incredible staff, I am in awe of my success as a speaker, business trainer, and spiritual success coach, and eternally grateful for the amazing clients I have all over the world.

I do not take where I am in life for granted. My success is not because of anything I did or deserve to have, but entirely because of God's grace, mercy, and favor over my life. I have practiced the principles of this book and simply put, they work. I am reaping what I have sown. How grateful I am for God's deliverance, from a life that was doomed by man's words- but redeemed by the Word of God.

~ Dani Johnson

"Pay attention and be ready to have your world rocked!"

~ Shandra V.

SPIRIT DRIVEN SUCCESS

F THERE IS one lesson in life I have learned, it is this; you never know when your life is about to change. You never know when one decision will dramatically impact your life and change your course of destiny. Are you standing at the crossroads in your life?

As I travel around the world doing training seminars and coaching business clients, I am truly amazed at the number of people who tell me they are standing at a crossroads. Most of them are searching to find something in their lives that seems to be missing, something that lets them know they made a difference in this world.

Are you struggling financially, physically, mentally, or emotionally? Are you trying to find your place in God's Kingdom? If you said yes to any of these, then you need to pay attention to this book.

While their present situations and personal stories are different in many ways, all appear to have one thing in common—they lost their dream and vision of what they were created to do.

Too many people in our society have settled for mediocrity. For one reason or another, their lives have been put on cruise control and with each passing day, an empty feeling continues to grow.

Maybe this is where you are at right now. Maybe you too are standing at the crossroads of life. If this sounds like you, if you can relate to what I am saying, I have an important message for you that will change your life.

My words are simple. Don't you dare put your life in a box! Don't you dare decide to settle for mediocrity! Don't you dare give up on your dreams! Don't you dare give up on your life! No matter how comfortable you are, no matter how much or how little you have accomplished in life, do not ever get to the place where you stop dreaming. Not just for yourself, but for the sake of your loved ones, for the sake of your spouse and for the sake of your children.

To dare to dream in the midst of adversity, in the midst of failure, in the midst of complacency, is to have hope. That hope, that dream, is a gift from God. It is His way of telling you that He has a plan for your life, if you will listen and give Him a chance to bring it to pass.

I know because God gave me a dream and He took if far beyond the limits I placed on it or could have ever imagined. I came from an environment growing up that had no hope, no dreams, no faith in what I could be; only criticism and condemnation of what I was expected to become. I came from an environment of verbal, emotional and physical abuse, a past that choked any dreams or hope I tried to have and labeled me with a life doomed for failure.

I look at the kind of mom I am today and I thank God that my home is the absolute opposite of the home in which I was raised. My God rescued me from my past, blessed me with an awesome family, and surrounded me with great people, great clients, and great friends, who have all made a massive impact on my life. I believe with all my heart that each one of us has been given unique gifts from our Creator and that each of us is called to put those gifts to a purpose in life.

In order for you to understand the principles of this book and what I'm trying to teach you, it's important that you understand where I came from to help you realize what I can do for you.

I hope you read the introduction because that explains my beginnings and the background I came from. If you're like me, you probably skipped the introduction and go straight to the good stuff, but please, go back and read my story so that you can appreciate what I'm about to share with you and understand why the principles in this book will radically change your life.

Through our businesses we have helped tens of thousands of people all over the world improve their lifestyles and finances. I have seen people healed emotionally, physically, spiritually and financially, while getting out of debt, becoming financially independent, and yes, even becoming millionaires.

Are you struggling financially, physically, mentally, emotionally, socially, relationally? Are you trying to find your purpose and place in God's Kingdom? If you are nodding your head in agreement, then please pay close attention to this book. Together we will explore how others have walked down this path and triumphed.

Is there an area in your life in which you are not satisfied? Is there something in your life that is not quite right? I'm talking about your life. I'm not just talking about your career or your business. Are you fully satisfied in your marriage? Are you fully satisfied as a parent? Are you fully satisfied as a leader in your community? Are you fully satisfied as a son or daughter of the Most High God? If you aren't, don't give up. Don't stay in a rut. Don't stay status quo.

Since 2003, I have helped thousands to wildly succeed in the marketplace and achieve financial freedom. In these very same 'business' seminars, where key principles of debt and finances are taught, I have also seen God's hand touch lives and change them forever.

I've seen miracle after miracle of documented testimonies. Here are just a couple of the lives that have changed:

- *Krisztina and Andy, who had lived together for 12 years, came to First Steps to Success and got saved during the weekend. Since then they were married, have quadrupled their income and they just bought their first property!*

- *Carman from Michigan came to one of my business seminars and, after learning key principles and business skills, went from making $700,000 a year to $3.7 million in just 18 months. She turned her life and business over to the Lord. She was radically moved by the Most High God, and she risked her business reputation, her relationship with her employees and customers and now boldly professes Christ in the marketplace. She could have lost it all and been labeled as a Jesus freak, but God continues to blesses her.*

- *Douglas from Georgia came to a 2-day business seminar with Dani and during the Spiritual Equipping Session, he and his wife watched his leg grow 4 inches! They both became believers that night and are raising their children in His way.*

Not only have I had the privilege and honor of helping my clients make millions of dollars, but I have also seen God's anointing on our seminars in the following ways:

*Marriages healed

*Millions of dollars of debt paid off

*Grooming children for success

*People set free from bondage

*Families restored

*Businesses quadrupled

*And so much more!!

I have seen the Spirit of God move in amazing ways. God planted the desire in me to equip the saints to succeed so that man does not control His people. I love Isaiah 61, it is my life scripture. It talks about releasing the captives and bringing the prisoners light and freedom.

Have you walked away from God? Have people let you down? I could spend hours telling you what the Lord has done for me and how He brought me out of a condemned lifestyle and set me on a path to free others. I pray He reveals to you, what His power is about, what His grace is, and what His blessing is for YOU.

So I ask this again; are you satisfied financially, physically, mentally, emotionally, socially, relationally?

If you can't say yes to one any or just one of those, don't give up. Don't stay in a rut. Don't stay status quo. God did not intend those areas of your life to be mediocre. Don't choose to live under your own excuses. I learned that it is never the circumstances, but it is how you choose to deal with the circumstances that determine the outcomes in your life.

You may not realize it, but there is skill, talent, and ability, that are sitting dormant in you, waiting to come out. If you are genuinely seeking to release these gifts, I want to give you a shortcut, a direct path to rediscover and awaken those gifts that have been buried inside you.

In this book, I can only point you towards the source of what guided me through some incredibly difficult times. This source is the only one that was able to penetrate my heart, start me on a new path, and bring me to where I am today. And believe me, I know. I've tried many different and misdirected ways to get at the truth.

The last thing I want to come across as is a Bible-thumping fanatic who wants to shove scripture down everyone's throat. However, I do want to tell you the truth about what happened to me, and how the God that is revealed through scripture has been faithful to all His promises.

Through the transformations I have seen in my own life and in the lives of my clients, I believe that the Bible is the greatest success book ever written. It is jam-packed full of wisdom, insights, and messages—God's direct communications with us.

I have read the Bible from cover to cover several times, and each time I am blown away at the treasures that are hidden in the stories, the situations, the characters, the Psalms, the Proverbs, and the Parables. Although each story in the Bible contains some obvious lessons, the real treasures are sometimes buried a little bit deeper.

My hope is that you will discover the mentor, coach, encourager, and loving Father God, who knows your heart and wants to satisfy your every need. Since I began my relationship with my Lord and Savior, He healed my heart and set me free to live a life bigger than I could have ever asked for or imagined.

If you are one of those searching to reclaim that true vision for your life, then it is time for you to find your path, uncover your true gifts, and step forward into the journey that God has planned for you.

It is time to turn your back on the life you lived before. It is time to turn your back on the things that have been holding you back. Set your sights on achieving a success wilder than you can even imagine and choose a path of higher calling—the path God intended for you.

Start living your life with SPIRIT DRIVEN SUCCESS.

Spirit Driven Success has been an amazing blessing to my life and my husband's life. Dani brings truth to the Word of God and what we as people should be doing to our lives, surrendering ourselves to Him and being the best that we can be according to His will.

~ Denise

THE BIG PICTURE AND YOUR PART IN IT!

I N DECEMBER OF 1997, I had just given birth to baby number four and was enjoying all that comes with motherhood and taking care of a family. Hans and I attended a church of about 2,500 people that was an hour from where we lived, but we enjoyed the teaching and that more than made up for the long commute.

One Sunday, our pastor got up and gave one of the most memorable sermons I've ever heard. He was grieved, when he said, "I am here today to repent." He continued, "All of you that are in business, please stand up." Hans and I stood up with the rest of the crowd. There were a lot of us.

Tears were streaming down his face and he said, "The Lord gave me a revelation that you have the same anointing I have. You are a king in the marketplace and we have prostituted this pulpit. We have sold this pulpit, saying that this is the ultimate success, but the Lord showed me that there are some called to be priests and there are some called to be kings."

As my pastor did this he asked us all to forgive him because of the corporate structure that was developed, what he did wasn't even scriptural.

My Revelation

I'm going to share something with you that had me confused for a very long time. You see, right after I dedicated my life to the Lord, I became very confused because I was a business trainer, teaching people how to become wealthy. Here I am teaching people how to build their businesses and yet believing what I'm teaching people is useless for the Kingdom of Heaven.

I began to think, now that I'm a Christian, I should go to seminary and become a pastor, because it's obvious that my gift is with people and that is what I'm supposed to do. Then again, I'm in California, I'm a woman, it is 1993, and I can't even think of one woman preacher at that time. Quickly I thought, "No, I don't think that's going to work," and yet, I really thought that was what I was supposed to do.

The church would say things like, "Hey, we need nursery workers, we need youth people, and we need, we need, we need, we need and we need." So, I'd say, "Okay, maybe I'll go serve in the nursery," and I would do things like that, serving here and serving there. But nothing felt right to me. Something was missing as far as what I did for God.

As time went on I began to feel more and more useless in the body of Christ. I was helping people in my business right and left. Marriages were being healed, families restored, people were making money, paying off debt, actually coming to me at a training seminar, but I felt useless inside. I felt like what I was doing must not be for God, because I'm not at a pulpit and I haven't reached the corporate ladder inside of the four-walled church.

I hadn't realized it but there really is this ladder to climb to the top in a church. I felt like a total loser because my butt was always in the seat and never doing what I really wanted to do, which was preach the word of God and share what He had done for my life. You have an anointing; you may be a pastor of your company, some an evangelist in the marketplace, but you have been made to feel like you are useless in the body of Christ.

You're going to receive a calling that's going to shock you, and your life is never going to be the same, as mine has not been the same for the last four years, since I got my mandate. No more separation between your God and your business. No more separation between church and the marketplace. Today is the day that all of this stuff is coming together and the true word of God is going to go out like a storm and take the Kingdom of Heaven with violence, as it is written in that Bible. I hope you're ready.

Distortion

There's no doubt in my mind that every man or woman that goes to seminary and every man or woman that feels the call of God to become a pastor has no intention at all to screw people up.

Anyone that has chosen that field loves God and loves people. At the same time, across the board, business and religious leaders have misled people everywhere. In positions of leadership everywhere people have been misled. Do you know what I'm talking about?

Sick and Tired

Eight years ago I retired from my business. I got sick and tired of selling the world in a pretty package. I got sick and tired of just talking about business all the time and teaching people how to make money. I looked into the Heavens and I said, "God, if I cannot use my mouth freely for You I will not use it at all. If I cannot tell the truth about money, I can't tell the truth about You and what You've done in my life, then I will shut this mouth and do nothing with it." And I did. I walked away from an outrageous amount of income, an outrageous amount of notoriety, and outrageous amount of thank you's and letters and cards and fame, and I said, "I'm done. I'm out of here."

After I quit I became a full-time mother and I realized I was miserable. It wasn't related to my mothering duties, I loved being a mom. There was a void in my life because I was denying what I love to do. Somehow I got this religious thing in my head that said, "You have five children. You're supposed to be a full-time mom baking bread, rolling out pasta, making homemade pies, making everybody fat and driving your kids crazy." I got that religious thing in my head that said, "You're a wife and a woman and this is where you belong, in the home!"

I do believe there are some women that enjoy that lifestyle and that's all they want to do. There are some women who think that's beautiful and wonderful—but that's not the mandate that God gave me. I love my children with my whole heart and I love training them up and

I'm proud of every single one of them, but I drove them crazy when I was home 24/7. I loved being a mom, but there was a thing in me that had to go out and make an impact on peoples' lives.

A New Mandate

Four years ago I got a mandate from Heaven. Do you know I believed that I would never speak again? Then God gave it back to me but this time it was renewed, refreshed and refined. This time I was ready "For such a time as this!" Hans and I stepped out into the marketplace and I said, "I'm only going to speak if I can tell the truth about my God and what He has done in my life." Now, here we are, over 100,000 clients in four years. I'm working part-time. That's all God, because He did it. He brought the people. He made it happen. He moved the heavens and the earth to make His will come to pass. He's looking for a peculiar people to raise up in the marketplace.

A Peculiar People

He's looking for a peculiar people to raise up out of the bounds of religion and straight into a walk with Him and Him alone, to do the mandate in which He has sent you to do. You are designed by The Designer who planted a desire in you to succeed. Not to be a nursery worker. I have nothing against a nursery worker, there are plenty of them. However, there is a mandate and there is a revival, and I'm going to tell you about it.

My husband comes home with this book, *God at Work*. Every

one of you needs this book. It's written by Rich Marshall. There's a volume one and two, you need them both. He came home with this book. I read the first three pages and wept like a baby because it was speaking to me. It was speaking to what was in me, something that had confused me for a long time.

Now here's something interesting, to me. Do you know what it says in the first part of this book? He was in the same exact church service that I was in! I was there in that seat, holding my three-month-old baby boy. The same service! What are the odds?

The preacher was impregnated with this message of repentance about the pulpit being prostituted and sold to be something that it's not. He goes out and he begins to anoint kings in the marketplace. He begins to raise people up. This is a book about the revival that's been going on in the marketplace for years. It's a book about men and women who thought, like me, that they were supposed to walk away from their business and become something that they're not. They failed, so they had to go back into the marketplace to get a job. Then they find themselves getting and making millions of dollars.

God shut every door for them to be a minister, opened every door for them to succeed in the marketplace, and encouraged their gifts of witnessing to the guy at the water cooler or praying for the person on the phone. Signs and miracles erupted in that company. You want the fear about making money as a Christian broken off of you? You'd better start reading this stuff. You can get God At Work, Volume One and Volume Two at GodisWorking.com.

After that I began to find purpose in what I did. First of all, I want to share something with you. Man, in all our frailty, in all our wanting to do good and be good but messed up from all different influences, doesn't understand unity. The truth is God's idea of unity and man's idea of unity are completely different things. We use 10% of our brain; how in the world can we understand an infinite God?

Man's idea of unity is total conformity; everybody looking the same, everybody wearing the same thing, everybody wearing the same exact shoes, everybody making sure that you show no cleavage, you're not wearing any jewelry, no makeup, etc... God's unity is not conformity. God's unity is absolutely diversity in harmony.

Somehow we have got it into our heads that this is a separate calling. We've gotten it into our heads that only the preachers preach the gospel, that only preachers are anointed to pray for the sick. Somehow we've got it into our head that only the super ooky-spooky rowootabakashasata people—only those people have the power and the authority to see God move. My Bible says something completely different. The devil was really ticked off when I found that book.

The Disconnect

There is a calling on your life, but it's sad and unfortunate that the puzzle that's been painted to you is separate from the puzzle that God has painted for you. You're a piece in a very big picture. I truly believe that 80% of the church is absolutely inactive. I have a book that proves it to me based on facts. You might want to get a hold of this book. It's by George Barna, *Revolution.*

He is a pollster who polls the United States and the question that he asked was, "Where do you get your influence?" It might make some of you sick to know the answers. There's a big disconnect. Sunday we do our little church thing; we act like our good ole Christian boy or girl, and on Monday we go do a different thing. We come back on Sunday and repent for the different things that we did Monday through Saturday.

Can you please tell me who on the planet is raising up people to succeed in the marketplace with Godly principals? There's a lottery message that's being preached, "Oh, well if you just sow into my ministry today, I just know, I can feel it, there's somebody out there with $1,000. Ooh, there's somebody out there with $1,000—ooh, I think there's somebody out there with $2,000. God is going to bless you if you sow into my ministry right now. Ooh, I see it. It's coming!"

We've all seen that and some of us have even written the checks. That's a lottery message. He who chases fantasies has poverty waiting for him. I'm not saying that every preacher that says that is not hearing from God. I am saying that if someone bought it because they wanted to get what was promised that was coming from a heart chasing a fantasy.

The Poverty Lottery God

The other message that's being preached from that place is poverty. Let me tell you why the lottery message does not work. Are you ready? *Because it nullifies the laws of success that are written in the Bible.* You cannot sow and sit, and expect something to happen. That's against the laws of success in the Bible. That is the message that's been going out there and it infuriates me.

My Bible says ask, seek, knock. Ask. Seek. Knock. Those are action words. It doesn't say ask, sit; it says, ask, seek, knock. So here we are, "I wrote a check so I'm waiting for my blessing." It's the same lottery message of this, "God's going to cancel your debt this year. I can feel it. God is going to cancel your debt this year."

Oh really? Who's debt is He going to cancel? According to what my Bible says, He is not going to cancel somebody's debt that's completely irresponsible and continues to be irresponsible because they will wind up in debt again.

According to my Bible, God gives you whatever you can be trusted with as it says in Matthew, "Because you have been trusted with this, now I will make you ruler over much. I'll give you five talents, you turn it into ten. You get to keep all ten. Now you go and make it happen again." That's what it says.

It says that if you can be trusted with what you have then you'll be given much. So we have a body of believers believing in a Fantasia God. That's called idolatry the last time I checked. So what do we have? Hope deferred.

The other message that's being preached is this; is that in order to be meek you must be broke, and there's not one place in my Bible where it says that. There's not one. I have searched, and if you need to know, you go search yourself. I have searched that thing high and low, studied it over and over again. Poverty is a choice. It's your choice. Are you going to follow the laws to succeed or are you going to follow the laws to fail?

There are keys to poverty and there are keys to wealth and they both come out of the same God. Unfortunately only one side is preached, only one message is given, and the message in most places is this, "Whooo, you better watch out because it's much easier for a camel to get through an eye of a needle than it is for a rich man to get to Heaven. Money is the root of all evil—be careful; don't get all caught up in that materialism."

The Deception

I was so deceived, and not by any man. I was deceived by the Devil, not by any pastor. You know what I believe? I believe that your Daddy loves you. I believe that He loves you and He loves the way He made you, and He made you for a unique and strategic perfect position. He made you for something specific. We cannot keep trying to fit into a box, whether the box is Christian or whatever religion you're in, or your box is over here, just business and I don't get to serve God because I'm not holy enough.

Let's say in a company there is a management position that is open and in that management position there are two people: one that says they are saved and they love God, and then there is another person who is a complete heathen, addicted to pornography, that is drinking and carrying on and full of greed and all this other kind of stuff.

The guy that's addicted to pornography is absolutely diligent and hardworking and does whatever it takes to get a promotion; and the one that calls himself a Christian, who has heard the lottery message, hears that there is a management position available and just says, "Well I'm just going to pray about it." He prays about it, but does nothing to increase his skills to ensure that they will get that promotion. He does nothing to co-labor with Christ other than chase a fantasy that says, "Well, I'm a child of God and He loves me, so that position is mine." Not if you can't do the work.

That's all the way back to Matthew again in the Parable of the Talents. The Bible says that He gave each according to their ability. Who's in charge of that ability? Do you have the power to increase your ability? Yes, you do.

All on your own? No. You're stupid if you try to do it all on your own. If you're smart you will ask an infinite God, a supernatural God, to give you supernatural strategies, supernatural abilities, supernatural favor in the marketplace with people, supernatural prophetic gifting that you would know things about people that you normally would not know so that you can speak into their lives.

So do you know what I believe? I believe that my Daddy in Heaven, as I am a child of God, as I am honoring Him, as I am tithing, as I am being trusted with what I've been given, that when I am diligent, hardworking, and showing myself to be faithful I am serving my Master.

A promotion. Who's going to get that promotion? Daddy's girl is getting that position. But I won't get that position if I am not doing my part. The lottery message is ask and sit.

I truly believe if there are two contractors bidding on a job, the one that serves the Most High God and that is diligent and works with the spirit of excellence is going to get the job. I believe that with my absolute whole heart. I believe those that are chasing a false God, this lottery God, are going to still stay broke and impoverished. Why? Because the Bible promises, "He who chases fantasies has poverty waiting for him."

I believe that if a contractor was to take the Holy Spirit on the job with him he'd be far more proficient than he is with his own hands. I believe wholeheartedly. You want to know why? Because I live this stuff.

The Joseph Blessing

Many times I find myself on my face, crying out to God for Him to move in peoples lives. Why? Because there is nothing I can do on my own. I'm crying out to Him, saying, "God, only You can satisfy them. Let them hear You, because there's no words from my mouth that are going to make a difference in their ears." I have seen Him move. I have seen Him give revelation. I have seen Him set feet to flight. So you better bring Him with you at whatever you do because He wants to bless the work of your hands, just like He blessed Joseph. He prospered Joseph in a prison. He prospered Joseph as a slave and a foreman. He blessed Egypt because of Joseph.

God is raising up Josephs in the marketplace right here and now, and it's just whether or not you'll be faithful, as Joseph was, to call upon His name that is above every name. It's whether or not you will call upon the gifting that He has stored up in Heaven. He wants to open up the storehouses and give it to you if you're willing to be diligent with what you've got already.

Has it ever once occurred to you, to ask God to give you favor? Has it ever occurred to you to ask God to bless you? Has is ever occurred to you to ask God to grow your business beyond your ability? Has is ever occurred to you to ask God to give you supernatural ability?

Do you know that's what I have done? Since I rededicated my life in 1993 God gave me supernatural ability. I'm telling you it's supernatural, because there is no way this former broke, homeless cocktail waitress who was saved by grace could do these things.

You were called for such a time as this and to open the floodgates, send His angels that they would bring you strong people for your business. Ask! God give me supernatural ability to hear and to absorb and to catch what I need to catch so I can run with it. Give me supernatural faith, God. I promise that whatever You plant in me I'll run with it. Did it ever occur to you that there is a revival going on in the marketplace and there are people lost and suffering and hopeless out in the marketplace that need a real touch from a real God? And do you not know that you have the right to ask?

Can I tell you a secret? Us and our little pea-picking brains, what we've done is we've limited an infinite God who has some funny ways of doing things. We have created this religion of how we feel He can operate. Isn't that pathetic?

Influence

What does a big business get you? Influence. What does influence mean? People are listening. People are following. Watch this. I mentioned George Barna's book *Revolution* and it's about where Americans today get their influence. Barna says, "There are seven dominant spheres of influence." By the way, this is not his opinion, these are the facts. This is through polling. This is through the testimony of the people answering the phone and the answer to the question of "Where do you get your influence?" Well, according to his documentation, the seven dominant spheres of influence are: movies, music, TV, books, Internet, law, and family.

The second tier of influencers is comprised of entities - not one person; an entity. Ready. Schools, peers, newspapers, radio, and business. The church didn't even make it in the top 20. So what does that mean? The church has no influence.

You might blame somebody or this, that and the other thing, but I'm going to tell you it's by design. It's by design that the top influencers are music and movies and business and radio and schools and Internet, because God is raising up a peculiar people that will infiltrate those very places and bring the Gospel straight to every crack and every crevice.

He is raising a people, a peculiar people. Read Joel 2. Read

Acts 2. You're going to find out what I'm talking about. According to the facts, not according to Dani's opinion, the church has become irrelevant for whatever reason. I promise you it's by design. God had a plan. There is no reason to lose hope because you are part of the hope.

The whole plan of church programs and buildings and build more buildings and bigger buildings and more programs and more programs, and get more volunteers and recruit more people has failed to take over our cities for God. The cities have been overcome by other influences. But let me tell you who has and always has had influence. Are you ready to find out?

Who Has the Influence?

The kings. This is the way it works in the Bible. You see, the priests served the kings, not the other way around. The priests served the kings. The priests were the ones, through relationship with that king, relationship with God, would hear from God and would bring direction and a message to the king. So who had the voice with the people? The king.

The king was the voice box to the people, not the priest. The same is true today.

The priest is supposed to—the pastor, the minister—is supposed to influence the king, raise him up, give him Godly advice, give him good direction, that they would be a light on a hill, that they turn to their place of influence and they shout from the mountaintops the direction from Almighty God. The kings have the influence in the marketplace.

Who's at the head of the Internet? The kings. Who's the head of books? Kings. Who's at the head of everything that I just mentioned, movies, music, all of it? Kings. They are leaders. Leaders are dominating the marketplace, and God is looking for a peculiar people that want to run with Him, that want to take the cities by storm. He wants a peculiar people that His anointing will be on for business, because business is one of the chief influencers in our cities and in the world today.

Are you in business? The kings have influence. Unfortunately, in a lot of places the kings are put down, they're belittled, and their anointing is not called out of them. It's more, "Be careful. Don't sin. Be careful. Material things." "Well, you shouldn't be driving that Mercedes." "Really? Gosh, that's kind of strange, because I was able to share Christ with the car."

Can I tell you a secret? God knows how to bait the hook. Get Him out of your tiny little box. Do you know how my God put my husband and me together? Lust!

We put God in this tiny little box. Now look at what we do. We wage war on the marketplace, sent by Almighty God. Do you want to know how God got me back to Him? Greed!

He knows what to bait the hook with. He's smarter than you and me. He's infinitely intelligent. He put greed on the hook that caused me to turn back to Him while I was losing everything and I needed help. "Salvage my company please, before I lose it all." It was absolute greed.

Do you put God in this tiny little box that says, "He'll only bless me if"? Get Him out of the box.

Holy Enough

My life is a living testimony of what I am sharing with you. I have found a God that has given me everything that I have and it has been for a unique purpose that completely is different than anything I would've ever thought it was for. It's much bigger than what I thought it was for.

Why in the world was I a broke, homeless cocktail waitress, who became a millionaire in two years? So you'd pick up this book and get this message. If I was still broke would you have read this book? He knows what bait to use.

The message, "You've got to be holy. You've got to be righteous." Can I tell you what's wrong with that message? I believe the heart is right, but I think the method is wrong. Man has preached that message as though holiness is something that you attain through things that you do or that you don't do. That takes God out of the picture. That again is idolatry.

Same with righteousness. The way righteousness is taught, as though it is something that you do or you don't do. You gain righteousness based on what you do or you don't do. I'm sorry, last time I checked my Bible, Abraham, who was a sinner, was called righteous.

Holiness is a direct result of submitting 100% of your life to Him. And it is the fruit that comes out of you as a direct result of submitting your life to Him. It is not based on what you wear; it's not based on what you drink or what you eat. Holiness and righteousness comes forth by the spirit of the Living Holy Righteous God. Man can't produce holiness or righteousness. It is not humanly possible. It is only possible by doing John 15, "If you remain in me, then I will remain in you."

The last time I checked an apple tree, in the season while

a bud was coming out the tree wasn't going "Aaaargh—an apple." The last time I checked, the fruit of an apple naturally comes out of an apple tree, because that fruit is remaining in the vine, or in that case the tree. An apple does not produce an apple by trying really really hard not to sin. Have you tried to become holy?

You become holy and you become righteous by remaining in Him. Out of His grace, mercy and His unconditional love, He then begins to produce it out of you. It becomes the fruit of who He is in you, not based on what you wear or what you don't wear, not based on the perfect language that you speak, not based on what you eat or what you drink or what you don't drink. It's based out of being with Him.

Are you tired of trying to become holy enough to be used by God? He loves you and He's going to use you the way He used the disciples. After the disciples failed Christ, after they denied Him, after they did not believe that it was Him in that room that appeared after He had risen, after they did not believe and said, "Let me see if that hole is real," right in that very same breath He said, "Now go and preach the gospel to all creation." He said, "Go. Heal the sick and cleanse the lepers." He said, "Go raise the dead." He said, "Go set the captives free. Go give them the gospel, the good news that I have risen and I have set them free" after they were screwed up, messed up, not holy, not righteous and not pure, and they didn't go to seminary.

A Peculiar People

The gifts of the Spirit have also been taught that they only exists within the four walls of the church. There's nowhere in my

Bible where it says that the gifts of the Spirit are for four walls. It doesn't say that. It doesn't say that the gifts of the Spirit are only for those that went to seminary. It doesn't say that the gifts of the Spirit are only for those that are pure and holy and righteous according to man's standards. It doesn't say that. It says that He's given them to all men.

All I know is God is raising up a new breed of people, a peculiar people who are called by His name to do some peculiar things. He is raising up kings in the marketplace because they have influence.

You are supposed to make money because money brings influence. According to this worlds standard, money brings influence.

Can I tell you what the three-fronted battle is? The world desires success, the world desires fame, the world desires power, they desire excellence. Why do we watch sports? It's excellence in action. Why do people go to the orchestra? It's excellence in action. Why do people go to operas? Excellence in action. The world desires these things.

God is looking for a peculiar people that will trust Him and that are called by His name, that will be risen up in those places of influence, of money, and power, and fame. Why? Because you will do what I do; you will point to the King of Kings and the Lord of Lords and you will say, "I got to this platform because I was saved by grace." You will say and you will testify what He has done in your life, just as I am testifying to you right now what He has done in mine.

He is looking for a particular people that will give Him the glory that He deserves. He's looking for a peculiar people that will ask for stupid things. Through my influence that God has given me, and the people He has planted the seeds in do you know how many souls have been won into the Kingdom of Heaven? Tens of thousands? I cannot count. We have no way of counting. We get emails all the time, people giving their lives to the Lord from the web site. We have testimonies of healings from the web site.

He is looking for a peculiar people that will trust Him, but will use what He has given them to say what? "He has saved me by grace and He has blessed me with everything I have. If you will serve Him, He will bless you too."

He's looking for a people that He will cloak in everything that the world desires. Because underneath the cloak, underneath the diamonds, underneath the suits, underneath the business success, underneath it all, is Jesus, the King of the marketplace.

Have you ever imagined you'd read this kind of message? God knew what to put on the end of the hook to get this book in your hands or get your butt in the seat at a seminar. Maybe for you it was greed. Maybe it was success. He knew what to put on the end of the hook to get you to hear that He's calling you by name, that He has a revival going on out there. There are people out there that are lost and suffering that need a real God and not religion.

The Battle

There's a two-fronted battle that you were called to fight. Let me give it to you.

1) The first fronted battle. **Making money is spiritual warfare** and here's how it works. Your heathen competitor, who would take those profits and use it for his own glory, use it for his own greed, and use it for his own gluttony, is no longer getting those profits, but instead someone that

God can trust with the profits is, that's you. Making money is spiritual warfare.

2) **Your influence**—You have a message with influence, as I am using my influence to give you a message right now. The second form of the battle is your influence in producing a message that people are hearing. And if you're wise and you're smart and you can be trusted with your mouth, that God would say, "If you will let me use you then I will speak a message through my people."

3) **Profits**—The profits that you're gaining on the front end in the marketplace that your competitor is not getting because you are being trusted with what God has given you, those profits now go where? Not into greed, not into pornography, not into excess alcohol, not into stupid things, but you're giving your 10% to the Kingdom of Heaven because that's what He requires.

Is the heathen competitor giving 10% to the Kingdom of Heaven? No. He's giving it to organizations that take all the glory for the help. We have given seven figures into the Kingdom of Heaven in the last couple of years. Don't think that's great about me; that's great about an intelligent God that would say, "I will trust you with money as long as you give Me My portion." Sure. No problem. That's a good deal. "You keep 90, I get 10." That's a good deal, don't you think?

Robbing God

Are you robbing God and not giving Him 10%? If you aren't giving 10% you can't call yourself a king. I'll tell you that right now, what you've got is going to be taken from you, because you can't be trusted with what you've got. If you're not tithing, you're in trouble. You're expecting to make money, but you're robbing God, you can forget it. Repent today and start giving.

You give not in the name of the Red Cross, not in the name of the Salvation Army, but in the name of Jesus.

Can you imagine a body of kings, people in the marketplace that are making an obscene amount of money that are living on 10% because they don't need 90%? Hans and I live on less than 10% of our income. Why? It's too much. We live on less than 10% and I get everything we need and more and that on less than 10%. We give far more because we don't need it all.

Could you imagine what would happen if you were willing to do what I'm telling you to do—you are willing to pray, you're willing to seek, you're willing to be diligent, you are willing to work with excellence, you're willing to give, you're willing to take the marketplace by storm and you're to bring excellence in the marketplace?

Allow me to share a personal belief. People all the time, Christians especially, say, "You are a Christian; you should do your seminars for free?" I'm sorry, my doctor's a Christian. Does he perform open-heart surgery for free? They ask because Christians, with the lottery message, have an expectation of poverty, which is getting something for nothing. We seek something for nothing. If you're seeking something for nothing, you're going to get nothing.

Crappy Christians

Why is it that anything that has a Christian label seems to be crappy? Can you tell me? My husband had a vision and this is what he said, "If we're going to do this we're going to produce the best possible training in the marketplace. And by the way, we're Christians. If you have a problem with that go somewhere else." The bottom line is you will not be able to deny the results that we get, because we went out to compete head-to-head with the blessing of God right in front of us out into the marketplace, and as we have gone out there with the best, not with halfhearted work, not with crappy training that doesn't work and gets no results. We have gone out with the best that we had to give. However when Christians start a nice little program it's like, "What can we do for really cheap? What can we cut corners on? What can we do for free?" Poverty. Poverty. Poverty.

A king competes head-to-head in the marketplace. A king goes and he takes new territory and new ground. A king goes into a city and transforms that city. Not by crap, but by excellence.

When Solomon built the temple what happened? He brought the best. He brought the best workers. He brought the best craftsman. He brought the best artists. He brought the best ironworkers. He did not get crap.

Could you imagine a group of business people that are making an obscene amount of money, that have far more than any they could ever have use for? Could you imagine having a business that you can walk away from for two straight months and could you imagine your income not even being touched for that two months, that the business continues to grow because God is the CEO of that business?

You could go and take supplies into a place like Africa or

Thailand. You could go and we actually bring miracles and not, "Just let me pray with you and teach you Jesus Loves Me, this I know, cause the Bible tells me so." People going in and teaching Jesus Loves Me songs, but what did you bring? "I prayed for some people." Awesome. They're starving. They need food. And you come with basketfuls of food in Jesus name.

I'm not discounting prayer. I'm not discounting Jesus Loves Me songs, but God is raising up a peculiar people. He is raising up kings in the marketplace that will make far more than they could ever spend, kings that can be trusted with that bounty, because He will send them into those nations and those places, and for two months we will bring our families into those places and we will feed the hungry. We will pray for the sick and they will be healed. We will bring miracles and supplies and we will bring wisdom and knowledge about how they can take care of their land. We will bring wisdom and knowledge that will teach them how to prosper right where they're planted because we know how to do it, that's what we do in the marketplace.

We come home, our business is just fine. God is raising up a peculiar people that are called by His name, that He will be glorified in their success, that He will be glorified with what they do, that will give Him the glory that is due to Him. He is raising up a people that He will send out to places like Thailand to free those captives in the sex trade.

We've been sending over $20,000 a month to a place that builds orphanages for babies. Do you think that's making a difference? Yes. I'm sure your $10.00 is helping too, but if you actually got serious and you realized that you've been called to go make a whole lot of stinking money, you can send something that is building shelter after shelter after shelter, that is setting thousands of captives free instead of just one. It's okay to send one. It's okay. But I think that we can do better than that.

The Bible says that money is the answer to everything. I didn't write that. You can argue with God about that. How are we going to take the marketplace by storm? How are we going to do this? We're going to do it with guerilla warfare. Conventional warfare says this, you see my ammo and my people, I see yours, okay, ready, 1-2-3 bm-bm-bm-bm-bm. Guerilla warfare says this: that I look just like them and I am sneaking into the enemy's camp, and before the enemy even knows, I've already set the captives free. Before he even realizes that they're gone, we are long gone.

How will this be done? Guerilla warfare. Where does He want us? Everywhere. Read Joel 2 again. He wants us everywhere, even in politics. Do you have a desire to be in politics? Where do you think that desire comes from? He wants us in politics. He wants us in music. He wants us on the television. Covert. Guerilla warfare.

People are tired of religion. They are tired of the traditional crap. They want excellence, they want success, and they want fame. Business, education. He wants us in the marketplace because that's where the people are.

The Great Commission

You're supposed to use your profession for the Great Commission. The Bible is clear about what we are anointed for and what we are called to do. Isaiah 61:1 is my life purpose. It says, "The spirit of the sovereign Lord is on me because the Lord has anointed me to preach the good news to the poor. He has sent me to bind up the brokenhearted, to proclaim freedom for the captives, and release from darkness for the prisoners." Have I not been preaching good news to the poor? That's what we're called to do. Our profession is to be used for the great commission.

Mark 16:15 says, "Go into all the world and preach the good news to all creation." John 20:21 says, "Peace be with you. As the Father has sent me, I am sending you." Matthew 28:18, "All authority in Heaven and on Earth has been given to me." Luke 10:19 says, "I have given you authority to trample on snakes and scorpions and to overcome all the power of the enemy. Nothing will harm you." Matthew 10:8 says, "Heal the sick, raise the dead, cleanse those who have leprosy. Drive out demons. Freely you have received, freely give." Matthew 17:20 says, "Nothing will be impossible for you." That is what we're supposed to do. We have been given the authority; we have been given the right, now go fight.

As kings there's a few things that you're supposed to be doing.

1) Giving—You are supposed to give.

2) Influence—You are supposed to influence people properly and point straight to Jesus.

3) Pray for the impossible—Walk towards your miracle. Don't sit and wait; start walking.

4) Take Risks—As a king you are to take risks.

5) Trust God—Trust God and not your ability or your talent. I used to trust in my talent and my ability. I no longer trust in either. My talent and my ability might be okay; however, my God's ability and my God's talent and my God's gifting are absolutely endless and only He can satisfy.

6) Pray for others—You see a need; you give your testimony about what God has done for you and pray for them, prophesied over them, encourage them.

7) Worship—Worship Him and Him alone. I've studied the kings in the Bible for about five years now. I will tell you the biggest mistake that they've made and the biggest thing that they have done to cause the anointing of the Lord to come off of them, the thing that they have done to cause the protection of the Lord to come off of them is they worshipped other Gods.

Greed is idolatry. Your talent, if you idolize it and your hope is in it, that is idolatry. If you have been worshipping this false god that says you're supposed to be broke and be nothing and no one, that is idolatry and it's time to repent. It's time to tear down the places of idolatry. Tear down the high places in your life.

Let me give you another one—"I can't make it. I can't do it. I will fail. I'm not supposed to be here." That is idolatry, because you are on the altar. Anything that exalts itself higher than the knowledge of God must be torn down. The reigning thought of "I can't make it. I don't have what it takes. I wish there was a different way. I wish they would give it away for free." You have exalted your knowledge higher than the knowledge of God that says, "I have called you." The knowledge of God that says, "Go ye forth into all the world and preach the good news to the poor."

Today you will repent for idolatry. You will tear down the high places; that is your mandate as a king in the marketplace.

8) Excellence—You are to produce the best that you can and compete head-to-head with the marketplace. You have the spirit of the Living God that is on you, that will give you designs, that will give you strategies, that will give you inroads, if you ask Him.

9) Seek God for everything—Seek God for everything. David inquired of the Lord left and right.

Proverbs 3 versus 5 and 6 says, "Trust in the Lord with all your heart. Do not lean on your own understanding, but in all your ways acknowledge Him and He will direct your path." That must be what your life is about. Because as a king, from much that has been given much is required. He will bless you, but you better stay nestled right up next to Him or you're going to get yourself into some trouble.

10) Act as a king—Heal the sick, cast out demons, bring sight to blind eyes, let the deaf hear set the captives free. That is your mandate from Heaven. That is your calling from Almighty God. He is raising up a peculiar people that are called by His name, that will succeed by His hand, who will be diligent and will be wealthy because of their diligence, because He promises that, a peculiar people that will go in every crack and crevice to reach somebody, a people that have a mandate to take the Kingdom of Heaven violently by storm.

"Prior to Spirit Driven Success™ I was totally lost. I had walked away from God and headed down a path of destruction. Then I heard Dani give a message of truth that taught me how to get back to God and recommit my life to Him. The Words she spoke broke the yoke of bondage in my life and I believed for the first time: "There is therefore now no condemnation for those who are in Christ Jesus." I am now experiencing God's amazing love, forgiveness and mercy. Dani has delivered a message that my soul longed to hear and I have received complete restoration in my life. If you've lost your way – get yourself Spirit Driven Success™ today and hear the message God has for you!!!"

~ Maraloo V.

THE TRUTH ABOUT MONEY

Y OU WILL NEVER enjoy total freedom without God. You must have God in your life to experience true freedom—that's the bottom line. Since you're reading this book, I know you are anticipating learning something that will change your finances and even your life. You may even have a hunger and desire to change in you, that you don't understand. Let me ask you this, "Have you been under a cloud of confusion concerning money?" Don't worry, you're not alone.

I think THE most famous quote about money that I've ever heard, is that "money is the root of all evil." Well I'm here to tell you that's a lie from the pit of hell! Nowhere in the Bible will you find the saying that money is evil. You won't find that.

In fact, my Bible says that money is the answer to everything. Are you wondering, how's that? Well Ecclesiastes 10:19 says that "money is the answer to everything."

Let me ask you this—what if I could show you that, according to the scripture, poverty and wealth is a choice? Your God-given freedom is to be able to make choices in your life, so which will you choose, poverty or wealth?

I can tell you this, there's no scripture in the Bible that says He made you for poverty. It doesn't say that.

Now let me tell you what it does say. "I have made them rich." "I made Abraham rich." "I made Isaac rich." If God designed you for poverty then why are most of the men and women in the Bible extremely, filthy, stinking rich?

Years ago after walking away from God and then coming back, I earnestly went before God and said, "You know what God? What can I do for you? I'm a business woman. I do business training seminars. I prepare people to do better in the marketplace. What in the world can I do for You?"

Let me tell you something. There is no disconnect in the Bible about what happens between God and the marketplace. There is no disconnect between God and what you do for a living. In fact, in Colossians 3:23 we are told "And whatsoever ye do, do it heartily, as to the Lord, and not unto men." That's what it says. This is only one of the many business references found in the Bible.

My husband and I once felt that disconnect too. We struggled to find our place and felt like total failures in the body of Christ. We felt that we weren't being used. We were going to our pastor and telling him what we could do and asking, "Can you use us?" Over and over we were told, "Ah, not right now. Maybe some day."

We had helped thousands of people in the marketplace make ridiculous income, healed marriages and restored families. Yet, when we presented this saying "Here's what we do and we'd like to help," we simply heard, "Why don't you volunteer?"

So, for years we felt useless in the body of Christ. What could we do for God? We didn't fit into the "traditional" structure of the church and felt we were not accepted for what we wanted to give.

Some day never came for us. Year after year, after year, we kept feeling hopeless and useless sitting in the pews paying our tithes (which I'm sure paid for somebody's salary). We experienced this huge disconnect. We were churchgoers but felt useless.

The largest revival in the world is happening in the marketplace right now. Here it is. This is fruit of a marketplace. God wanting to meet you right where you are.

God has set a divine appointment for you. Why? Because there are too many of His people that are held captive in a pew doing nothing with their gifts and their callings and what they've been prepared from the day of their birth to do. They're not using their gifts because there isn't a place in the corporate structure of the church. Are you called to full time ministry as a traditional minister?

There have been many times where I've felt like, "Okay, I better volunteer for God." God has given each and every one of us a gift and we're to utilize it and prosper, which is what I am going to show you how to do.

Think about this; have you ever asked yourself, "What can I do that's purposeful?" If you have a strong desire to make a whole lot of money, once you understand God's desire for you to be wealthy, is it possible that God would have a purpose for that money?

What do people say about money? You have one half of our culture that says, "Get it, get it, get it, more, more, more, now, now, now, now." Then you have the other side that says, "Oh no. Be careful. Ouch. Did you see them? They're driving a Lexus. Oh God have mercy on their soul." Maybe you've prejudged someone. Who knows, maybe they live on 10% of their income and they give 90%.

You see greed does not have an amount. Let me say that again, Greed does not have an amount! Have you ever looked at the wealthy and prejudged them for being wealthy? Maybe you've even thought, "All those wealthy people are power hungry idiots. They're greedy people and don't deserve to have that much money." If you've ever thought or spoken those words, you may not realize it but in judging others you've judged yourself. In cursing others because they are rich, you curse yourself.

How can God give you wealth if you yourself, have cursed the wealthy? If you have said or thought that about the rich, you have an issue you need to take care of. Not only do you need to seek forgiveness for thinking that way, but you need to stop saying those negative things and deal with your heart issue about passing judgment in the first place.

It's easy for people who are broke, especially Christians, to judge the wealthy and use the scriptures to justify their finances. Check your heart and make sure that isn't you.

God's Financial Kingdom

Whether you know it or not, there is a financial Kingdom. The people who succeed in the financial Kingdom, for the most part, are following the rules. But I have found that you can even follow a few of the rules, mess up on a few, and God's grace is so sufficient that He lets you try again, and again, and again, and again. In essence, Life is just one big fat test.

Poverty vs. Wealth

There are two extremes in the Financial Kingdom: poverty and wealth. In the Book of Proverbs (22:2) it says, "Rich and poor have this in common, the Lord is Maker of them all." Rich and poor, the Lord has made them all.

What if I could show you that you have a choice of which one you can be?

Have you figured out you've been in the poor line? I know what that feels like because I grew up poor. My mom was on welfare. I was on welfare when I was 18. Now check this out. This is very powerful. The Bible says clearly that He is the respecter of no person. He shows favoritism to no one.

Do you think that the wealthy have some kind of favor? That God has shown favoritism to the wealthy? If they're blessed like that, they must be God's favorites right?

If God is not a respecter of anybody and doesn't show favoritism to anyone that means it's an equal playing field, right? Then what does the financial Kingdom, and everything for that matter, boil down to? It boils down to you and the choices you make. *The fruit of our choices show up in our finances.* Did you catch that? *The fruit of our choices show up in our finances.*

Let's look at both sides of the financial Kingdom so that you will be able to see clearly, and I mean ever so crystal clear, which side you're on and if necessary, how you need to get to the other side.

Proverbs 28:22 says, "A stingy man is eager to get rich and is unaware that poverty awaits him." Now here's the deal. Sometimes we're stingy and don't realize it. How do you know if you're stingy? Look at your fruit. How do you know what kind of seed was planted? Check out the fruit. What causes poverty? Stinginess and hoarding. Stinginess is a poverty mentality.

So is stinginess a choice? If you choose to be stingy you choose to be poor—by choice.

Proverbs 21:17 says, "He who loves pleasure becomes poor."

Why? Think about it. One that loves pleasure will spend everything they have to get instant pleasure.

Proverbs 17:2 says, "A man of perverse thought will not prosper." What is perversion and what does it have to do with the financial Kingdom? "A perverse thought" could imply the perversion of truth, as in, "The love of money is the root of all evil" being perverted into, "money is evil". But a "perverse thought" can also be found in other areas of your life where you've taken something pure and twisted it for pleasure or immoral purposes; pornography, adultery, illegal business dealings, etc...

The Bible talks about meekness. Specifically, it says that the meek will inherit the Earth (Psalms 37:11, Matthew 5:5). Man has perverted that scripture to mean that you must be poor to be meek. That also is perversion.

Proverbs 28:19 says, "He who works will have abundant food but the one who chases fantasies will have his fill of poverty." Twenty-five percent of this great nation's plan for financial independence is the lottery. Can you believe that? A poll asked people, "What is your plan for financial independence? What is your retirement plan?" Twenty-five percent of the people responded, "Winning the lottery."

Proverbs 6:9-10 says, "How long will you lie there you sluggard?" I love this scripture. "A little sleep, a little slumber, a little folding of the hands to rest and poverty will come unto you like a bandit."

Let's continue. Deuteronomy 28:47-48 says, "Because you did not serve the Lord your God joyfully and gladly in the time of prosperity, therefore in hunger and in thirst, in nakedness and dire poverty, you will serve the enemies that the Lord sends against you." Wow this is a powerful verse—think about it. Think what God is warning you about. And it is a warning. During a time of prosperity,

God wants the glory. He wants you to bless Him. It shows throughout history and throughout the scriptures that God, before time of repentance, would ravish His children with great prosperity to turn their hearts towards Him.

His first method was to bless abundantly so that they would just fall to their knees and say, "God we don't deserve this. Thank you Lord for what you've done. Your goodness is overflowing. Your grace is more than sufficient. Your mercy just completely blows my mind." Unfortunately, He never heard these words.

Instead, they got full of themselves and greedy for more, more, more. Have you ever been hungry, thirsty, and naked, in dire poverty serving your enemies? I have and it stinks.

Proverbs 13:18 says, "Ignoring discipline causes poverty." Do you need to be a little more obedient?

1 Samuel 2:7 says, "The Lord sends poverty and wealth." Did you think it was man? The Bible says, "The Lord sends poverty and wealth." The Lord sends it. He humbles and He exalts. He raises the poor from the depths and lifts the needy from the ash heap. He seats them with the princes and has them inherit a throne of honor. Do you want to be one of those that He exalts? Then there are some things that you have to change to avoid poverty.

Okay. Let's talk some more about money. Here are some scriptures that reference the negative side of money. I am sure you already know these. You've undoubtedly heard them your whole life.

Matthew 6:25 says, "No one can serve two masters, either he will hate one and love the other or he will be devoted to the one and despise the other." You cannot serve God and money. And that's the truth. You can serve the God who has the money. Yes, you can.

Ecclesiastics 5:10 says, "Whoever loves money never has

money enough." That's, by the way, how you know if you're plagued with greed. That's how you know if you have greed in your heart. No matter how much you make it's never enough. You are never satisfied with what you have. That is called having a spirit of greed. I was once absolutely plagued, possessed by a spirit of greed and I'm here to say that there is no price that someone can pay me to do something that my Daddy in Heaven has not led me to do. Nothing. I will not compromise my walk with Him for a price tag. Ten years ago, totally different story.

"Whoever loves money, never has money enough." The rest of Ecclesiastes 5:10 says, "Whoever loves wealth is never satisfied with his income. This too is totally meaningless." Are you completely satisfied? It probably never seems to be good enough, right? No matter what you do, every time you hit a goal, it never seems to be good enough. Do you feel that you're constantly falling short? Be honest with yourself. If you're never satisfied with things, possessions and money, then you're plagued with greed.

Greed is a wicked, wicked, wicked deceiving, crafty, evil spirit that will make you do things that you never even thought were possible to do. That's if you've submitted yourself to that spirit of greed. So if you don't have enough, it's only going to hurt you.

Proverbs 13:11 says, "Dishonest money dwindles away but he who gathers money little by little makes it grow."

Acts 8:20 says, "Peter answered may your money perish with you because you thought that you could buy the gift of God." There's a rich man in the Bible that wanted to buy a spiritual gift. That's something you can't buy. Spiritual gifts only come from God. You can only seek them from Him. You can't purchase them.

First Timothy 6:10 says, "For the love of money…" Go ahead; I know you want to finish that statement, "…is the root of all evil." The love of money. How do you know if you love money and you love wealth? If you're never satisfied with it. If it is a deep hole within you that never seems to be filled, that means there's a spirit of idolatry and you are worshipping that God instead of the Almighty Himself.

Now here's the positive side of money. Ecclesiastes 7:12 says, "Wisdom is a shelter as money is a shelter." Ecclesiastes 10:19 says, "A feast is made for laughter and wine makes life merry but money is the answer to everything." This scripture sets the record straight. "Money is the answer to everything."

How's money the answer to everything? The Book of Matthew says, "Again it will be like a man going on a journey who called his servants and entrusted his property to them. To the one he gave five talents of money. To another he gave two talents of money. To another he gave one talent. Each according to his ability."

According to each one's ability. He gave one five talents, another two, and one received only one. Each according to what? His own *ability*.

So check this out. Did you know you can increase your ability? Who's in charge of increasing ability? You are. You're in charge of increasing ability. So if you increase your ability in the marketplace, you will prosper greater for the new ability that you bring to the marketplace.

That's what the Bible says. But what we have is people waiting for something to fall out of Heaven to make them wealthy. That, my friends, is a fantasy. You've got the name it and claim it generation. "Just claim you're wealthy" are the words they are holding on to. "Just claim your prosperity." Claim it without working for it is nonsense and is a fantasy and poverty awaits you. That's the truth.

So, Proverbs 17:16 says, "Of what use is money in the hand of a fool since he has no desire to get wisdom." Money without wisdom is only going to lead you down a path that you don't want to go.

So, let's talk about wealth. I can pull up a whole bunch of scriptures about greed. Colossians 3:5 says that, "Greed is idolatry." That's what it is and to be quite honest with you we live in a nation that has more idolatry than any other nation on the face of the planet. Our idolatry is far more crafty than the idolatry in India.

So here's the deal, idolatry is ramped. We admire song writers and singers. We, idolize sports figures. Your kids have little idols in their toy chests, action figures. They do. We've got idolatry all over the place. We teach our kids idolatry and we don't even realize it. If we don't get it straight, we have got a spanking coming from God.

A greedy man brings trouble to his family, but he who hates bribes will live. Proverbs 28:25-27 says, "A greedy man stirs up dissension but he who trusts in the Lord will prosper. He who trusts in himself is a fool, but he who walks in wisdom is kept safe. He who gives to the poor will lack nothing."

I'm going to say that again. "He who gives to the poor will lack nothing." If a person is stingy, will they give to the man on the street? No. If you're stingy, will you pour into charitable organizations?

If you're currently not giving to someone, you my friend are stingy. And what follows stinginess? Poverty.

The passage goes on to say, "But he who closes his eyes to them receives many curses." Luke 12:15 says, "Watch out. Be on your guard against all forms of greed. A man's life does not consist in the abundance of his possessions." Where does greed lead? It leads to poverty. It leads to wickedness. It leads to destruction. It leads to all those things. Can you enjoy wealth without being greedy? Yes. Absostinkinglutely.

Listen to me carefully. What is it about us that we somehow make greed and wealth the same thing? You can you have wealth without being greedy. Do you want to know what perversion is? It's labeling all wealth as greed. That is perversion and what does the Bible say about perversion? A perverse thought will be impoverished.

Is it possible to be wealthy? Yes. The Word says, "God created the poor and the wealthy."

7 Steps to Poverty

I pointed out several scriptures in the Bible that explain poverty. I have searched every single scripture, every single scripture that talks about being poor and poverty and there are about seven reoccurring themes.

So here's a formula for poverty. Seven steps to poverty.

Step 1—Be lazy and half hearted. So, be lazy and work half heartedly unto yourself or unto your boss. Let me say that again? Work half heartedly to yourself or to your boss and there is a guarantee that poverty awaits you.

Step 2—Become a fool, drunkard, glutton or a wasteful people and you will go poor.

Step 3—Have pride during times of prosperity, forgetting God and that will bring on poverty.

Step 4—Hide your sins. There's a scripture is Proverbs that says, "He who hides sin has poverty waiting for him." Basically, if you attempt to hide your wrongdoing you will realize poverty.

Step 5—Love money and that will bring on poverty. If you desire money more than you desire anything else, more than God, more than your kids, more than your wife, then guess what, poverty will show up at your doorsteps.

Step 6—Be selfish and stingy. This is an absolute formula for poverty. People that do not give will be impoverished.

Step 7—Be fearful and poverty will come on you.

In Matthew 25, the Word talks about the Parable of the Talents. Matthew 25 talks about the servant who said, "I was afraid so I hid my talent" and God called him wicked and He cast him out with weeping and gnashing of teeth. The servant says, "I was afraid so I hid my talent," which meant he did nothing with what was given to him.

If you do nothing with what God has given to you it will be taken away. This could be your business, maybe the job that you have, the family that you have, the responsibility that you have. If you do nothing with the talents, if you're called to sing and you're doing nothing with it. It will be taken from you and given to someone else who already has, and you'll be cast out.

God's Formula for Wealth

So, what is God's formula for wealth? Let's go through some scriptures and find out.

Deuteronomy 28:53 says, "It pleases the Lord to make you

prosper." What? It says that it pleases the Lord to make you prosper. Do you have kids? Doesn't it please you to bless them, especially when they've done something good? Of course. Your Daddy in Heaven, who is perfect, and who is unfailing in His love, desires for you to prosper. If you're not prospering, you've got to ask yourself, "Why not?" Deuteronomy 29:29 says, "Follow my commandments so that you may prosper in everything you do."

Follow my commandments. Don't murder. Don't steal your neighbor's wife. Don't be greedy for other people's things. Don't lie. Don't cheat. Don't steal. Is that something you can handle?

Proverbs 11:25 says, "A generous man will prosper." Proverbs 28:25 says, "He who trusts in the Lord will prosper." Jeremiah 29:11 says, "I know the plans I have for you, plans to prosper you and not to harm you, plans to give you hope and a future."

Ezekiel 36:11 says, "I will make you prosper more than before." Daniel 4:1 says, "May you prosper greatly." Genesis 39:2 says, "The Lord was with Joseph and He prospered him greatly." Deuteronomy 35 says, "He will make you more prosperous." Job 22:21 says, "Submit to God and be at peace with him; in this way, prosperity will come to you." That's what it says.

Do you know there are even more scriptures supporting wealth and money than there are those talking against it? So, there are essentially 10 steps associated with God's formula for wealth.

10 Steps to God's Formula for Wealth

1) **Don't love money more than you love your God.** If you are all consumed about money, if you worry about money that means that money is an idol to you. If you worry about money, you worry how you're going to pay your bills. You worry about how you're go-

ing to take care of the mortgage. Guess what? That is money being ahead of God.

The word of God tells us to take every thought captive to the obedience of Christ. In Matthew 6:25-34, it says (paraphrased), "Do not worry about what you will eat or what you will wear because your God in Heaven already knows what you need". There is no need to worry when you have faith. So if you're worried about money, guess what? That's nothing but a total deception from the pit of Hell.

The enemy wants you to worry about finances, wants you to think about money to drive you away from God because he knows that if you actually follow Him, if you actually honor Him, if you actually love Him, if you actually serve Him, God will prosper you and make you great in the city gates. So you'll be blessed going in and you'll be blessed coming out. He will bless those that bless you and He will curse those that curse you. The enemy of your soul knows this. Why? Because he reads the Bible more than you do. It's the truth.

2) Work with a spirit of excellence as unto Him. That's what it says in Colossians. It says, "Work with all your might unto Him."

Would you say that you need some work in that area? Probably. But if you work your business with all your might as unto Him, He is your boss. And when it comes time for promotion it does not matter what a jerk of a boss you have ahead of you because God is over him or her. And guess what?

He sees what you do. He sees your diligence. He sees the extra hours. He sees the motivation. He sees the heart that you're pouring into it. He sees and will bless the fruit of your hands. Don't worry about your boss. God will just promote you right above him.

Look at Joseph in the Bible. His story is so powerful. Joseph is blessed by his father with a vision, and then thrown into a pit. He is then enslaved, brought to Egypt to be a slave in a governor's house who worships a foreign god, and the Word says that God prospered him. He is then accused because of an adulterous wife. "Ooh Joseph, come here honey." She looked at that fine young man and said, "I've got to get me some of that."

And Joseph ran. He eventually gets falsely accused of committing adultery and is put in prison. God exalted him from prison to become the head of the most powerful nation of that time.

So, you have nothing to worry about. It doesn't matter what man or woman is above you. That means nothing because God will bless the fruit of your hands. That's if you are working it as unto whom? Him.

3) Know that the money that He is blessing you with is for a much bigger purpose than just your stuff. Does that mean that God wants to bless you with stuff? Yes He does. But He doesn't want the 'stuff' to own your life.

My Heart to Heart With God

I was a woman whose stuff owned my life. Hans and I were living in this huge 6,000 square foot house, in our 20's and making a fortune. Life was good and everything felt like it was wonderful.

One day I was preparing for a Bible Study and the spirit of God came over me and I hear God say, "Who's this all for?" I started thinking, well it's not for my husband because he could live in a shack and be happy. "Then who's it for?" And I'm thinking God is speaking to me so I can't lie. Well God, it's not for my kids because they don't need 10 acres. They don't need a tennis court. They don't need a guest house. They don't need a 6,000 square foot house.

"Well then who's it for?" Hmmm...I was running out of options. My cheeks were twitching. "Then who's it for?" Well Lord, I guess You don't need it. You own everything.

I had tricked myself into believing that it was to honor God. I was convicted. I'm sorry, Lord. It's all about me. All my stuff, my cars, my jewelry, my clothes, my house was all about me and my ego trip. In truth, it was the lifestyle that this homeless cocktail waitress had accumulated and it was nothing more than a reflection of my big, fat, greedy ego trip. That's all it was. And you know what? I was empty inside.

No matter how much we made it was never enough because we spent faster than we made it. Here I loved God. I served God. I honored God. We paid our tithes. But it was all about, "Well this is what I'm accustomed to. This is the kind of lifestyle we're used to."

In a single moment that all changed when the Lord said to me, "Sell your belongings and follow me". Funny thing is I thought I was following Him. And instantaneously I said, "I rebuke you devil in the name of Jesus, go back to Hell where you belong!" He said, "This is Jesus and if you love Me, you will follow Me and you will sell your belongings." I started weeping and fell on the floor and began to cry and repent because I realized that my whole life had become centered on me.

I went downstairs to tell Hans what God had just said to me and there was my husband, sitting at his computer. He took one look at me and could tell something dramatic happened. He could just tell this was going to be a long conversation and he had this, "Don't bother me right now, I'm busy", look. So I go to him with tears streaming down my face and said, "Hans I've got to talk to you." He said, "What?" I said "This is serious. God just told me that we need to sell the house."

Now we had just moved into the house three months before. We bought the house in a down market in an area that is not prosperous for real estate. We saved $300,000.00 by moving up to the mountains and we got so much more than what we needed. When I said, "Hans, God told me we need to sell the house." His jaw dropped and he said, "God told me the same thing two weeks ago but I told God He'd better tell you because I ain't fighting that fight."

As God is my witness that is exactly how it went. Hans said, "You better tell her God because I ain't fighting that battle!" So here we were in absolute agreement, broken before God. And do you know how faithful God is? Here He exposed the greed that had crippled my life, and I hadn't even realized that I was walking through life crippled. I used to say I could walk away from this tomorrow and that it meant nothing to me until the day God told me to walk away from it.

But do you know what He did? Do you know how faithful He is? I told you that we bought the house in a down market in the area that is not prosperous for real estate. It had been in a ten year slump at the time. And do you know what the Lord did? He brought me one buyer who needed to sell her house in order for her to buy my house. She raised four children in a house that was built by a man who had raised four children. The land was totally set aside for God. These were Godly people, a Godly man had built the house and a Godly woman lived in the house and here she has to sell her house in order to buy my house. In six months there was only one person that came to buy my house and it was her.

She was going to turn my dream house into a board and care home for developmentally disabled people. Okay. Now this is what I'm showing you. God Almighty is so loving and so faithful that here He tells us to sell this house and what does He do? He prospered us in our obedience.

And He will prosper you if you're willing to work for it. He brought us one buyer who had a house that I hated but I knew walking into it that it was priced well under $50,000 on the market. I knew it was. I knew to just paint and put my stuff in it would raise the value instantaneously. Of course, I had to sell half of my stuff. My bedroom, I have scars on my toes from stubbing them in that stinking little closet. The new bedroom was smaller than my closet. Would you say that's humbling?

God in all of His love and His grace and His mercy; me while I was full of sin and greed and disgust and wickedness, we made $100,000 on that house. God sold that house. We bought it. We lived in it for 11 months and that was it. And we made $100,000 in a down market. The house that we bought currently has $150,000 of equity in it and is now a rental house being rented by Godly people that God is working on as well.

I remember talking to my sister-in-law who used to complain about the house she lived in. I said, "I know exactly how you feel but this house in this neighborhood has been the best thing that has ever happened to me because it was in this house where I was set free from greed."

It was in this house that I discovered every wicked, nasty, spoiled rotten brat thing that was in me. It was in this house that God set me free from something I had no idea I was in bondage too. And even now today when I came out of retirement and we started speaking again, we had companies offer seven figures so that I would only train for them because they did not want my mouth to continue being their competition.

"Dani, we'll pay you a million dollars a year. It'll be great. You will not have to build your own business. We'll just give it to you monthly if all you do is go on the road once a month for us." And now I could look them in the face and say "Thanks, but no thanks." You might be thinking, "You are stupid".

No matter how much we made it was never enough because we spent faster than we made it. Here I was. I loved God. I served God. I honored God. We paid our tithes. But it was all about us. This is the kind of lifestyle we had grown accustomed to. Wouldn't you say that was a humbling experience?

4) You have to know that it's God's money. It's not yours. It's God's money. It comes from Him and there's a much bigger purpose for that money. He wants to multiply that money, but when you get it and you don't honor Him or you're stingy with it or you're all caught up in it, He will not bless you with more. Why? Because you're on a road to destruction. If you're on a road to destruction, He's not going to give you more so that you wind up destroying your life.

5) Be generous. Don't hoard. Don't be stingy. God wants to bless you with more, but He won't unless you're a giver. He loves a cheerful giver.

We teach our kids to tithe because we don't want to deal with adult children that won't do what the Financial Kingdom calls them to do. So our kids tithe their own money, their own earnings. My daughter, Arika often works with me. She will take 10 percent of what she earns and give it to God. Do you want God to trust you with more? Then give willingly. Give graciously. Give with a cheerful heart.

6) Give into the right soil. This is absolutely enormous. When I first learned this, my head just about exploded. In the Bible, it talks about the Parable of the Sower. It talks about four different types of soil into which a farmer will sow. There is the rocky soil. If you sow seed on rocky soil it says it sprouts quickly because it does not have a root system. But it says that it gets scorched by the sun. It sprouts quickly and it dies quickly.

The second type of soil discussed is hard ground. With hard ground, the birds of the air come in and steal the seed away. The third soil is the thorny soil. This type of soil gets roots. As it pops up, it is choked out by the worries of life. That's thorny soil so it eventually withers and dies.

The fourth type of soil is fertile ground and it is the only soil that in which you want to plant your seed. The Bible says that on fertile ground there is a return of 30, 60 and 100 fold. Some of us are planting money in infertile soil. It says that whatever you plant then you shall reap.

Have you noticed that your income hasn't increased? Maybe it stayed the same. You have to think about where you are sowing your seed. You might ask, "How do you know where the ground is fertile?" You have to look at the fruit. If you want your money to return back to you a hundred fold, you have to sow it into fertile ground.

7) You need to realize that there is a time of plenty and a preparation for a time of famine. There are seasons of famine and seasons of plenty. That is absolutely scriptural. Joseph did this when God blessed his nation for seven years with great abundance. Are you in a season of plenty? If you are, know that the season of plenty is not for you to eat all your seed.

That season of plenty is for preparation so that you may still prosper when other people are failing all around you financially. So in the Book of Genesis we see very clearly how God has designed it.

If you're in a season of famine and you are prospering where you're planted and you can be trusted with what you have, you will gain more. That's how the Financial Kingdom works. If you're in that season of famine, you better take care of everything you have. Have a spirit of excellence unto and during this time He will cause you to prosper when other people are failing financially.

Remember what we learned earlier? The Bible says that if you forget Him in time of prosperity, poverty awaits you around the corner. So if you are in a prosperous situation right now, don't you dare forget who owns it and how He has blessed you.

8) You have to prosper where you're planted. Do you have dreams and visions of where you want to go and what you want to do? Are there places that you'd like to visit? Have you gotten frustrated because your dreams haven't come to pass?

Let me tell you, that is a plan from the enemy to get your focus on what you don't have instead of focusing on making yourself prosper right where you're are. This is how people do it. They have a dream. "Dani, when I have this big business then oh, I'm going to lavish my people and I'm going to take really good care of my customers. But these lazy, broke people, I can't stand them. They're driving me crazy."

Or I might hear, "Oh Dani, if my husband would act right I would do a lot better. If my husband would act right then I'd treat him better. If my wife would stop nagging then I'd buy her flowers once in awhile." It doesn't work that way. You have to prosper where you're planted under the current circumstance that you're in.

Joseph in the Bible had a gift to interpret dreams. He used that gift in a prison and that's what got him promoted all the way to the top overnight—because he prospered where he was planted. Was serving in the prison what he was designed to do? No, but during the time in the prison he was equipped to run a nation, the most powerful nation at that time.

9) You need to ask and ask big. Come on. God is not a small God. It says that His arms are not short and His ears are not deaf. The Bible clearly says that no mind has conceived, no eye has seen, and no ear has heard what God has in store for those who love Him.

You need to think bigger than what you're thinking. You need to think wider and taller than what you're thinking. And you need to ask in the way of God's size not your size. I'm asking God for millions of lives from all over the world. That's what I'm asking for.

"God please let me have the platforms where I can affect millions of people's lives from all over the world. That it won't stop there but, that they will go and they will affect millions upon millions of people's lives. That millions and millions of homes will be made right and come into right standing with you and principles that work." Also, part of Step 9 is you need to ask for help. The Bible says if you need wisdom to ask for it. If there's something you don't know how to do, ask and He will give it to you.

10) You need to understand that it is okay to fail. Its okay to make mistakes. There are ups and there are downs. In the down time, don't worry. Don't fret. Don't freak out. Just know that you are fully taken care of, that He loves you. And God will cause you to prosper. There will be rainy days. There are times you're going to make mistakes and I want you to write this down: <u>It's okay if you mess up.</u> It's okay. Why? Because God's word says that His grace far exceeds the Heavens. That is huge. His grace is enormous.

The only understanding of grace that we have is grace that our friends or our family shows us, and that's pretty pathetic wouldn't you say? A small amount of God's grace reaches the Heavens. The Word says that grace is never ending, which means that we have the grace to fail and to fall right into His arms. That He will brush off your knees put you back on your feet again and say its okay. Go at it again. How awesome is that?

As I mentioned previously, in all of my sin, in all of my greed, God still blessed me financially. Why? Because He is looking for an obedient heart that will fall into His arms instead of depending on their own. That to me is absolutely awesome.

I painted a picture of a Financial Kingdom. A Kingdom that spreads far and wide, but the head of that Kingdom is God.

Will you submit to Him so that He may bless you, that He will prosper you as He wants to prosper you? He desires you to be in good health.

God wants to see His people get out of bondage, financial bondage. God does not have a desire for you to be in financial bondage at all. Are you tired of financial bondage? Do you want to be free from it? Then you have to commit your ways to Him.

"I learned to forgive and bless those who offend me."

~ Annette Z.

RECEIVING GIFTS OF THE SPIRIT

HAT I AM about to share with you is something that I've studied and studied. The more I studied it, the more I came into this monster revelation. It has completely changed my life. I would not be here today had I not learned this particular truth.

I spent many years as a Christian businesswoman feeling completely insignificant in the Kingdom of Heaven. I felt like, "Okay, I'm a speaker, so I must get into some kind of ministry. That must be what I'm supposed to do." However, every time I attempted to try to do something for God, nothing ever opened up. As I shared in the last chapter, the church never gave me a platform to speak on, not even at a stinking woman's retreat, of all things. I felt so out of place.

My husband also felt out of place. We didn't feel called to the nursery. We didn't feel called to the children's ministry. We didn't even feel called to the youth ministry. There was no place for people like us. God prospered us greatly in the business world, filled up conference rooms with people for us to speak to and yet, I would have gladly done a Bible study for nine people.

What I bought into was I was never going to be good

enough for God; I wasn't pure enough for God, I wasn't holy enough for God, I wasn't righteous enough for God, and that God could never use me. I just was not called to spread the Word in which I so passionately believed.

Through my business I had the chance to lead a whole lot of people to Him, and to help a lot of people get back on track with Him. God gave me the chance through my business to talk about something that I am the most passionate about, and that is my God and getting people on track with God and making their lives right; following principles that really do work.

The principles that I share about success are in the Bible. You don't have to serve some man or some fake god to be able to get the things that you want. The One and true One wants to deliver you from that poverty. He wants to deliver you from that sickness; He wants to deliver you from whatever bondage it is that you're going through.

Yet, I always felt there was no place for me. Have you ever felt that way? Have you ever said, "There's no place for me in (you fill in the blanks)"? I said to God eight years ago, "God, if I cannot use my mouth for your glory, I will not use it at all," and I went back to folding my arms.

If I cannot tell the truth about success, if I cannot tell the truth about money, if I cannot tell the truth about God, then I don't want to use this tongue to speak about anything. It's not worth it for me. It's empty. I lived in the big fancy houses, had big jewelry, big clothes, big everything, just a spoiled rotten brat, and it was empty.

So the long and the short of it is this: It was my dream to be able to stand and tell the truth. To be able to just speak on our own platform, not be controlled by any company or any church leader, not to have anyone control the message. It is what it is, and if they don't like it, they don't have to come back, and I don't care because they're not my provider. My God is, and that's the way I saw it.

So what I truly believe beyond a shadow of a doubt is that the church has done a great job, but in the last days has become irrelevant in some places. The pulpit has been the thing that has been promoted. Meaning, "Well once you really are super spiritual, then you'll be able to speak from the pulpit. When you become very holy, then you'll get the title of Reverend or Pastor." That was what I was so working towards. "If I get good enough, then someday I'll be able to be that."

I was striving for something to which I wasn't called, not realizing that maybe God had a different plan for me. Let me challenge you here. Is it possible that there is a revival going on in the marketplace? Oh, there is. You're in one and you don't even realize it. Is it possible that God is looking for a chosen people, a chosen generation after His own heart, to be used in a mighty way out in the marketplace? Yes, because many business people wouldn't be caught dead in a church. I was one of them. Too many have been badly wounded by the church. Sad but true. They've been held back, not fed, just used.

Have you have ever been wounded by the church? Now I'm not bashing the church. I love my brothers and sisters, but the reality is they are people just like the rest of us, and people make mistakes. Unfortunately most people look at people in church and think, "Well, you're supposed to be perfect." That's our fault for even thinking that. That's stupid. We shouldn't have those kinds of high expectations of them. Should they live by a higher respect level? Yes, they should. Do they make mistakes? Yes, they do.

Anyplace you put people you're going to find mistakes.

That's the reality. So it's not up to us to look at the church and say, "You should be more perfect. You should be more holy. You should be more of this." No. You should step up and say, "I'm going to give it my best shot wherever I'm at"?

The unfortunate thing and something that my husband and I are very passionate about is there's very little equipping for people like you and I who are out there in the war zone every single day. How do I, as one that loves God, serve Him in my work? Is it possible that The Designer has made something for you to do out in the marketplace? Is that possible? Let's see what the Bible says.

When I rededicated my life to the Lord, I thought, "What's my use?" As I stated in Chapter One, I felt totally insignificant, like there was nothing I could do for God. And as my heart grew more and more in love with Him, my desire to move in His will increased and the gifts of the Spirit grew. The more insignificant I felt, the more I felt like, "I'll never make it to this position. I was never called to preach every week to the youth. I never felt called to the nursery wiping butts." I just never felt called to any of that stuff, and my husband and I felt insignificant, and almost guilty, because we felt like we were not serving God with what we were doing. I felt like I would never make it through their "corporate structure."

What is it about man that he has this little box over here called, "religion"? Do you know what the word "religion" means when it is translated into Greek? Bondage—return to bondage. Religion was created by man. It is man's ideas of how people should look. God's idea of unity and man's idea of unity is different. Man's idea of unity is everybody needs to look the same; look a certain way. Man's idea of unity is conformity. It says in my Bible that I am to conform to the image of Christ, not to the image of man.

Yet, what we've done is we've taken that Bible with our own

selfish motives, and we've put people in a box called "religion." We've put them in this little place and said, "You better look like this... dress like this... Dani, you shouldn't say stuff like that you're going to get in trouble." Where does it say that? Show me where there's sin in what I'm saying. No, there's truth in what I'm saying—sometimes the truth hurts.

God's Gifts to the Church

Have you ever felt useless? That your gifts and your talent have no purpose? If so, it's because we men and women have created this false structure; a structure that does not exist in the Bible. We've created walls to act out our spirituality and those walls need to come down.

Those walls need to be dozed, as they say it where we come from. It is time to pull the dozers out because there are too many captives that think that they have no talent. There are too many captives that think they are useless. What can you do? I'm going to show you.

In 1 Corinthians 12, we learn about spiritual gifts and our role in the body of Christ. This passage is not an exhaustive list of the gifts of the spirit (we will examine the 15 gifts and their position later), there are things listed that you have, and that you don't know you have.

1 Corinthians 12:4 reads, "There are different kinds of gifts but the same Spirit. There are different kinds of service but the same Lord. There are different kinds of working but the same God works all of them in all men." Who is all? Don't you qualify under all?

1 Corinthians 12:7-11 says, "Now to each one, the manifestation of the Spirit is given for the common good. To one, there is giv-

en through the Spirit the message of wisdom; to another, the message of knowledge by means of the same Spirit. To another faith by the same Spirit. To another, gifts of healing by that one Spirit. To another, miraculous powers. To another, prophecy. To another, distinguishing between spirits. To another, speaking in different kinds of tongues and still to another, the interpretation of tongues. All these are the work of one and the same Spirit and He gives them to each one just as He determines."

Verse 14: "The body is not made up of one part but of many. If the foot should say, because I'm not the hand, I do not belong to the body, it would not, for that reason, cease to be part of the body. And if the ear should say, because I'm not the eye, I do not belong to the body, it would not, for that reason, cease to be part of the body. If the whole body were an eye, where would the sense of hearing be? If the whole body were an ear, where would the sense of smell be? And in fact, God has arranged the parts in the body, every one of them, just as he wanted them to be."

Doze the Walls, Come Out of the Box!

Romans Chapter 12 says, "Just as each of us have one body with many members and these members do not all have the same function..." Man's idea of unity is everybody looking, acting, walking, talking, and dressing the same. That is an ignorant, foolish philosophy because man's idea of unity is conformity and conformity is a disease.

However, God's idea of unity is simple to figure out. Nothing is the same on this planet. Our DNA is different, our thumb print is different, and the hairs on our head are different. Grains of sand, grains of grass; nothing at all on this planet was created exactly the same. Even identical twins are not the same.

God's idea of unity is diversity in harmony. We just read it. "And these members do not all have the same function." I'm not supposed to be the same as everybody else and neither are you!

Have you have often felt that you are a square peg trying to fit in a round hole? Have you felt that you were different from everybody else? Perhaps you've even been told that you're different from everybody else? It's almost like a putdown but the reality is, it was by design that you're not like everybody else. The people that try to put you in a box are ignorant, foolish, uneducated morons. They don't get it.

You can look everywhere and nothing's the same. I can't find two pairs of jeans that are the same. I can't get two meals in the same restaurant that are the same. Have you come across people who have tried to change you? Have you had people in your church, whatever religion you serve, try to change you? You will be set free because I'm done with this nonsense. I'm done with it happening to me. I'm done with it happening to my fellow man.

"We have different gifts according to the grace given to us. If a man's gift is prophesying, let him use it in proportion to his faith. If it is serving, let him serve. If it is teaching, let him teach. If it is in encouraging, let him encourage. If it is contributing to the needs of others, let him give generously. If it is leadership, let him govern diligently. If it is showing mercy, let him do it cheerfully."

Ephesians Chapter 4, verse 11 says, "It was He who gave some to be apostles, some to be prophets, some to be evangelists, some to be pastors and teachers. To prepare God's people for works of service so that the body of Christ may be built up until we all reach unity in the faith and knowledge of the Son of God and become mature, attaining the whole measure in the fullness of Christ Jesus."

Now, please don't get me wrong. I am not bashing the

Church. I go to church. Every Sunday that I'm in town, I'm sitting in a house of worship. However I will say that it was created by man and man's ideals. Initially, man wanted to help, but I would have to say that we are a bit off track. We've turned church into a place, what I call a brick factory. We've made it cookie cutter—"if you're going to be spiritual, this is how you will act. If you're going to be spiritual, then this is how you will dress."

First of all, the Bible says, "He gave gifts to all men" and who is all again? That's you. Exodus 31:3 says, "I have filled him with the Spirit of God with skills, abilities and knowledge in all kinds of crafts." God has given you abilities.

Remember what it said in Matthew 25? "To one he gave five talents of money; to another, he gave two; to another he gave one, each according to his ability." Each according to his own ability and you own the ability.

Well, God gives ability with an expectation that you will increase your ability. Have you ever increased your ability before? How do you do it? Get to work? Get more education? Learn from a master? Gain more knowledge? Gain more expertise? Make some mistakes? Learn how to do it right? Now can you tell me if you have ever increased your ability before? When you increase your ability you profit more with that ability.

I believe we got off track because we have created these four walls. Do you feel like your gifts have been useless for God? Let me show you something in Romans chapter 12, verses 4 through 8. "Just as each of us has one body with many members, as these members do not all have the same function, so in Christ we who are many form one body. Each member belongs to all the others. We have different gifts according to the grace given to us. If a man's gift is prophesying, let him use it in proportion to his faith." Does it say that the gift is prophesying in the church? Does it say only on Saturday or Sunday in a building located for and only used by those who go to Bible College?

Let's continue with Romans chapter 12. "If it is serving, let him serve. If it is teaching, let him teach." Again, does it say in the church? "If it is encouraging, let him encourage." Does it say only in the church? "If it is contributing to the needs of others, let him give generously." Only in the church? It doesn't say that? Come on, there must be a footnote.

There must be some scholar somewhere that wrote an addendum at the bottom of the page that said, "This is only for the church." No? Wow, let's keep going.

"If it is leadership, let him govern diligently." In the church, right? "If it is showing mercy, let him do it cheerfully."

Romans Chapter 12, verse 8 says, "To one there is given through the Spirit the message of wisdom." Wait. Through the what? The Spirit. It doesn't say through the church as in 'building'. Something must be wrong with my Bible. It doesn't say through the church? It says, through the Spirit. You can get that message of wisdom.

"To another, the message of knowledge by means of the same Spirit. To another, faith by the same Spirit. To another, gifts of healing by that one Spirit." There must be something wrong with my Bible because it doesn't say through a priest, through a pastor, through some super intergalactic special from out of this world person with a green bellybutton. It doesn't say that? It says, through the Spirit.

"To another, the gifts of healing, by that one Spirit. To another, miraculous powers. To another, prophecy. To another, distinguishing between Spirits. To another, speaking in different kinds of tongues." Only in a church, right? Some are kings, some are priests. And yet, we have come from situations where stories have been twisted to put the focus inside the four walls of the church. And if the enemy can keep our thinking inside of the four walls, we are not a threat to the kingdom of darkness.

If our mind can be focused, that I have to serve only in the church, that I have to contribute only in the church, that I can only prophesy in the church and that I can only go to this guy to learn how to do those things, then what fear does the enemy have of you? Am I preaching to the choir? The message has been twisted by Hell. If we can only work in the gifts if you are super high up in the corporate structure and we can only use it in the building, that's a perfect plan from Hell to make sure 90% of the body of Christ is irrelevant.

It doesn't say that those gifts are intended for four walls. It also didn't say only for those in Bible College. "It only says by one Spirit." You might have missed the part. "Just as He determines." Did you see anywhere in there that said you can only use these gifts at seminary? That you can only use these gifts at church? That you can only use these gifts on the mission field" Where does it say to use the gifts? There are no boundaries. We have a boundless God, who works all these gifts for the edification of the body of Christ.

Kingly Anointing

David was not a pastor. The guy loved to kill people and yet he was the apple of God's eye. He was anointed king at the age of 16, but it was many more years before he became king on the throne. When he was first anointed king, he had to serve a wicked, stupid, immature, impatient king named Saul, but David refused to dishonor him. He submitted to the headship and he honored that king wholeheartedly.

God tested David and trained him, in his youthful days, on how to rule. His first submission was to a king that he did not agree with and God knew if this young man could submit to someone that he did not agree with, he'd have to instead honor him. God knew that David would honor Him.

"He inquired of the Lord…" David says it so many times in 1st and 2nd Samuel, it's unbelievable—"David inquired of the Lord." In Psalms, you see David whining, you see him rejoicing. He cried out to God for absolutely everything. He cried out to God for marriage advice, kid's advice, wars, battles, strategies, finances, and political issues. He inquired of the Lord on every single step that he ever took; he sought God in everything he did.

Every time he sought God, God gave his enemies into his hands. Do you have any enemies? Are you trying to fight them on your own? If God can take a 16-year old that can single-handedly kill a bear and a lion, and a giant, why in the world are you trying to do it by yourself? That is stupidity. You're not supposed to.

You may have been taught that God doesn't have time for you, that you're not supposed to seek Him for those little, tiny battles; that you can handle it on your own. I'm sorry. David asked for absolutely everything. God, what do you think? Should I attack now or should I wait? Should I go yonder, should I go to the west or should I start in the east? What do you think I should do? God would show him exactly what he was supposed to do, and his enemies were defeated.

Baptism by Bikini

I was in Belize not too long ago and the Lord brought this young man across our path. He spent the entire day with us; an 18-year old kid. He makes great money, bought his first house and a condo in Belize. He is blown away by my children. And he starts to ask questions. I said, "God has really blessed us." He looked at me cross-eyed like he had never heard this before. Long story short, by the end of the evening, he got saved. I told him that just the week before I was with one of my best friends who had got saved and baptized in my pool just a few days after. And he says to me, "You baptize people?" I said, "Dude, anyone can baptize people. John the Baptist didn't go to seminary to learn how to baptize. They didn't have it back then." The young man was like, "Oh, well baptize me." To which I replied," Sure. Ocean or pool?""

At midnight, July 4th, I baptized him in the ocean. He came out of the water baptized and slain in the Spirit. He gets baptized in the water and all of a sudden, he's saying, "Okay, when can I be baptized in the Holy Spirit?" So, I told him about getting baptized in the Holy Spirit right then and there. He said, "Really?" I told him "Yea, just say this." And then he starts, boom! He and all of a sudden, clunk! He gets hit by the power of God and his head goes back and it seemed like he was drowning.

God is my witness, my daughter Arika is my witness. He asked "What happened? I feel like a new person." I told him, "You are, you are dude!" with tears running down my face.

Anybody can baptize anybody. We have turned this into some kind of religious act and some kind of a corporate structure. You've got to graduate and take this test and do all this kind of stuff.

John the Baptist, under current, modern-day rules and regulations, would have been shot. Oh, wait a minute, I'm sorry; they cut his head off back then, didn't they? He didn't fit the mold. He didn't dress right, he didn't talk right, and he didn't act right. He did not know the right people. He did not come from that fandangle fancy church. He did not have a Certificate of Ordination. They would have slaughtered him in today's society, under today's rules and regulations. They would have called him a false prophet, slandered him and belittled his credibility, ignoring his anointing.

He ate bugs, he was a full-on tree hugger, a naturalist, a vegan. He was a homeless man, for goodness sakes. Do we have these standards? Not only that, he did not tell them what they wanted to hear, but he told them what they needed to hear and that was repent, walk away from your wicked ways and prepare the way for the coming Lord. They responded by cutting off his head because of that message.

I am about to get political here and I am not going to have any apologies. The truth is that we have fallen asleep. The truth is, there are millions of drops of innocent blood being shed right here in this nation every single year.

There's judgment and jealousy in our religious leaders. There's judgment and jealousy in us. While we're fighting out our stupid little doctrinal issues, innocent blood is being shed. Government has gone awry and wickedness is all over the land. Where are the Isaiah's? Where are the Jeremiah's? Where are the John the Baptists? Where are the Micah's who are not afraid to say, "We have screwed up and sinned against God?" We need to humble ourselves and pray. We need to do something about this and it's time for us to repent. We don't do that, instead, we have lots of fluffy words.

God's going to do this and God's going to do that. Yeah, that's great. But until we repent, He isn't going to do squat. You go and read that whole Bible. The bottom line is that until we turn our hearts wholly to Him and we repent for our actions, we ain't going nowhere.

Joseph was not a traditional minister. I don't know what it is but whenever God's message is preached, it's preached in a way that puts the 'old greats' of faith in the box of traditional ministry within the traditional four walls.

Joseph was a business man. We have created idols in our Bibles that are false. They were marketplace people who rose up in their calling, in the marketplace. There was no church. He was a little shepherd boy, the least in his family. Brothers hated him. He was full of pride. He would say, "God gave me a vision. You're the loser, I'm going to win." Oh, God had to discipline him.

Joseph has a vision that he knows is going to happen. He then tells it to the wrong people; moral of the story, don't cast your pearls before swine. So his brothers turn against him, they throw him in a pit and sell him off to slavery. He's then brought to Egypt and what does he do when he's there? Yes, he prospers. He uses his abilities and he prospers from them. He learned skills. He learned laboring skills. He learned construction skills. He learned how to become a foreman.

He applied himself to everything he learned. He got better. He applied the ability; God gave him more ability. Then he's promoted up to the governor's house. He learns in his house business skills, money management skills, people skills, leadership skills, real estate skills. This is what he's learning as he's being groomed by the governor. Can you see it? He had this dream that he's going to lead his little tribe. But God had something else in mind.

So in the midst of slavery, in the midst of bondage, Joseph was falsely accused and sent to prison. What does he do in prison? He prospers. Why? Because he took the business administrator skills he learned in the governor's house and applied them in the prison, gained more abilities, more favor, and then winds up being promoted from a slave to a ruler.

So in reality, the dream was actually smaller than what the reality of it was. Do you have a vision? I will tell you that your vision will test you. That vision will prepare you for what is to come. If you don't use your abilities, then you will fail and be called a wicked, lazy, servant. So let's talk about this.

Something else Joseph refused to do is he refused to bow down to their idols? God used a young man. Can you imagine Joseph under today's standards, according to the religious world? You're a Christian? You should not have a tattoo. Joseph was tattooed. He wore make-up. He dressed like an Egyptian. He walked like an Egyptian, he talked like an Egyptian. He ate like an Egyptian; he even slept with an Egyptian.

Colossians 3:23 says, "In whatever you do, do it as unto the Lord." How would you define "whatever"? What's everything? These are nice, generic terms. Your business, parenting, marriage, ministry, whatever you do, do it as unto the Lord. Your schoolwork, your profession, your trade. It says, "Whatever."

Have you heard this in terms of whatever you do is always context for the church? It doesn't say in the church. It doesn't say in ministry. Your ministry is whatever you do as unto Him. I do everything as unto the Lord. Why? It glorifies Him and it blesses people.

Discovering Your Gifts

Let's get back to Romans because we're going to look at all 15 gifts that the Bible talks about, that are given by the same Spirit. You're going to discover yours. You're also going to discover the gifts of other people. How can you use these gifts and how do they work in the marketplace? Are you interested in any of that? I know you are.

1) The Gift of Prophesy

Romans talks about prophesying. I've studied prophesying; I've read what it says and even looked it up in the dictionary. Throughout the Bible, it says to strengthen, it's for exhortation, edification and comfort and encouragement. That's what the definition of prophecy is in the Bible.

So when you look up those words, you follow the trail of what those words mean, encourage is to give courage; to give confidence or hope; to reassure, inspire, urge, support, advance, promote. Have you ever done those things? Exhortation means to urge strongly, earnestly, persuade. Many attorneys have the gift of prophecy. And they don't know it. Have you ever noticed attorneys paint a picture? They have a gift of persuasion. The gift of persuasion falls underneath the gift of prophecy. Are you good at persuading? That is a gift from heaven.

The gift without training leads to destruction. When you don't know you have the gift of prophecy, and who gave you the gift, and what you're supposed to do with it, you use it for the wrong reasons. Strengthen means to reinforce, renew, bolster, fortify, confirm, intensify, invigorate, nourish and rejuvenate. Have you ever done those things? That's a gift of prophecy.

Edification means to improve, enlighten, and bring guidance. Do you do that in your profession? A lot of teachers have a gift of prophecy. Prophecy is forth telling, speaking it out. Oftentimes, people who are prophetic get visions, they get pictures, and they get dreams, and then things happen.

Have you ever had that happen to you? Where you see something with your day eyes and then it happens? Have you ever gotten this hunch on something and all of a sudden, it happens. Have you ever driven by an area and all of a sudden, you sense an accident is about to happen and then lo and behold, right before your eyes there it is. That's a gift of prophecy.

Treat those that are around you as though they are all ready. When you do that, the prophecy comes to pass. The Bible says to use the gift of prophecy in proportion to your faith. Ask for more measure of faith.

2) The Gift of Service

The second gift is serving. Are you a nurse? You have the gift to serve. In the food service business? You have a gift to serve. It just comes natural to you. Where there is a need, you have a natural desire to fill the need. If something needs to be done, you have this natural desire; I'll take care of that. I'll be glad to. And you actually find satisfaction in helping other people. Is that you? That's a gift by the Holy Spirit.

3) The Gift of Teaching

Teaching is the next gift. That can be teaching anything. Does it say teaching only the Word of God? Let's see what the Bible says. "If it is teaching, let him teach." In the church? Let him teach in seminary? Nope. Do you teach? That is a gift and a calling from God, but somehow we have twisted it to fit inside of the four walls.

Have you ever noticed that you've been framed? We have been framed to think that all of that is only for the four walls. Do you have a gift to teach? You can't help yourself. Let me tell you something. Do you know that's a high call? You are passing on wisdom, knowledge, and experience that you've gained. You're passing it down to one who is unlearned.

4) The Gift of Encouragement

Number four, encouraging. This is calling out the destiny of someone else. For some reason, you see good in people. For some reason you see good in bad situations. Is that you? If so, that's a spiritual gift of encouragement. Does it say only encourage the people in the church? No. What does it say? "He who has the gift to encourage let him encourage." Where are you supposed to encourage? Everywhere, because it says "whatever you do." Whatever includes everywhere.

5) Contributing to the Needs of Others

Contributing to the needs of others is a spiritual gift. The Bible says, "Let him give generously." Why is it that we come from places that put down making money? That's a forked tongue. We come from places that put down money and yet the Bible says, "He who has the gift to contribute to the needs of others, let him do it generously." That means you have to have something to contribute. It's talking about money. If you don't have any money, can you contribute it?

We also see that people who contribute are put down because they only contribute money. "Well, fine. You just give money, but where are you serving?"

My husband felt like a bad Christian his whole Christian walk because he was money motivated. Every time there was a call, for example, the nursery needs workers, he was like, "I don't want to do that." He had no desire to help at all in any of their functions and he felt condemned because of it. Finally one day he said, "you know what, God? This is the way You made me, so You're going to have to deal with me. If You want me to change, then change me." God didn't change him. God stirred him even stronger to make more money. He even had him focus on learning new skills in computers, programming and understanding marketing. When he got free from the shame that had been put on him through condemnation, he finally started seeking out and increasing his skills.

Then guess what? The Lord gave him a revelation. That's his calling—to make a lot of money. Why? We give it away to people who are helping people. We give it away to the people that want to love on the babies in Africa. We give it away to people who have orphanages here in the United States of America for abused children to the tune of hundreds of thousands of dollars. Thank God, my husband got set free, otherwise he'd still be a boring, unusable man of God, which actually would be called wicked, lazy servant because his gift was not released. In fact, his goal is to give away one million a month.

6) Leadership

The Bible says, "Let him govern diligently." I don't know what it is, but the people who have the gift of leadership, they just seem to rise up. Joseph rose up, David rose up. Is that you? No matter where you go or what you do, you seem to rise up? Does it say lead as a church leader? Does it say lead as a mission leader? It says, "He who as a gift to lead, let him govern diligently." That means that this was designed and the gifts were given and designed to happen everywhere, not just this little place.

Do you have a gift of influence, a gift of leadership? Do you always seem to wind up in leadership roles? That's a gift from God.

7) Mercy

The seventh gift is mercy. The Word of God says, "Let him do it cheerfully." You have a heart for the hurting. You have a heart for the needy. When people are hurting, you're hurting. You'll do anything to rescue. You'll do anything to help. You will lay down your life for somebody else. That's a gift of mercy. Are you as compassionate as I am? Gift of mercy. You want to see restoration? You want to see redemption? You want to see reconciliation? You want to see families healed? That's a gift of mercy.

8) Message of Wisdom

1 Corinthians 12:8 says, "to one there was given through the Spirit the message of wisdom". You don't know where it comes from but all of a sudden you open your mouth and something smart flies out. You say, "That was really cool. Where did that come from?" That is the Spirit of the Most High, God. You open your mouth; you're like, dang, that was good. I have to write that down.

Does that ever happen to you? That's the Spirit of the Lord coming on you, giving you a message of wisdom. Have you had that happen and people tell you to shut up? Have you had that happen to you and people reject the message? I have but the message isn't mine; it comes from above. I didn't make this stuff up. You have a problem with it? Talk to Him.

A lot of accountants have the gift of wisdom. Analysts and engineers also have this gift. Have you ever seen these people operate? My husband has a monster gift of wisdom. It's amazing. We say in our office that Hans has seven brains because there's no way that much could fit into one head. All the different dimensions that he thinks in are unbelievable. Does this sound like you? It's a gift of wisdom. God gave you a different brain and it's amazing.

9) Message of Knowledge

A lot of counselors operate in the gift of knowledge. This is how the gift of knowledge works. You may come into the under-standing about someone's past. You may know the person but not know their past, or you know the person but for some reason, you get a message in your head about them.

Word of knowledge? You don't know that person. Don't know anything about them. For some reason, you see something. For some reason, their face is speaking something to you. What's going on in their heart, with their desires, whatever. And the Lord gives it to you and you say it to them and they usually respond, "How did you know that?"

I experienced something similar in Australia. There was this guy. I asked him, do you drive a red car? He's like, "Yea." I don't know the guy. Never met him before; don't know if I'll ever see him again. He asked me, "How did you know that?" I then proceeded to give him a message from God and it was dead on. That's what is called a word of knowledge.

Has that every happened to you before? That's the Spirit of the Most High God coming on you to deliver a message, a word of knowledge. When you don't know that you have the gift, you don't use it.

10) Faith

Faith is risk-taking. Faith is obedient to a vision. Faith is answering a calling. Faith is stepping out with no guarantee. Faith is believing whole-heartedly in the unseen. Faith is having the im-pression and urge of promise and then eagerly stepping out towards it even if it doesn't make any sense. Even if it doesn't look like it's going to work.

Here's what I know. He makes a way where there is no way. He uses the foolish things to confound the wise. It says that "we are the head and not the tail." We're going over and not under. We are above and not beneath. He makes crooked ways straight. It takes the gift of faith to follow what I just said. That's what it says.

Today Abraham would be considered a nutcase by most Christians because he heard voices; "Leave your father's house." He complains; but my dad's a rich man. Come on. I've got servants, I've got cows, I've got sheep. Man, I've got it all. But he obeys and leaves anyway and everything dies. The sheep are dying, babies are dying, women are dying and men are dying. The crops have failed. There's a famine in the land. That was faith in the unseen.

God says, "I will make you a father of many nations so your descendents will be numerous as the stars in the sky and the sand on the ground."

It says in Hebrews that "Abraham's faith was attributed to him as righteousness." So when you step out in faith to build your business, when you step out in faith to speak what is unseen, when you step out in faith to walk as though it is already; it is attributed to you as righteousness. That's faith. There is no faith in what's comfortable. There is no faith in what is easy. There is no faith in what is normal. There is no faith in the status quo. There is no faith in what's usual. That is not faith.

Are you an entrepreneur? You have the gift of faith. If you have stepped out, borrowed money as an investment to invest in a project, that is a gift of faith. If you have stepped out to find some investors who will believe in your project, that is the gift of faith. Have you stepped out and done really stupid things with no guarantee? Hallelujah, praise God. It's attributed as righteousness. Not all the stupid things you've done, but some of them. That is the gift of faith.

11) The Gift of Healing

There are lots of different ways that healings happen. The Lord gave me this revelation years ago and man, I crumbled. I absolutely crumbled and repented on behalf of our entire nation for this one.

For some reason, certain sects of the church only count divine touch from Heaven healing, as God healed me. They don't count what happened with Hezekiah. King Hezekiah was sent to a doctor. A doctor came, gave him a prescription that healed him and he lived 15 more years. In this nation, our doctors have taken the glory of God away by the confession of our mouths.

"I had cancer. I had to go through chemo." No, you would say, "I had chemo". Notice, that was a healing. God uses different ways to heal. It's shown throughout the entire Bible and yet the doctor gets the glory when it's surgery. The doctor gets the glory if it's chemo. I fell on the floor in my office, crying out to God saying, "Lord God, please forgive me on behalf of our whole nation who has exalted the ones You've given the gift to heal instead of glorifying You, The Healer."

If you have been healed, and I don't care about the modern day drugs, who do you think inspired the pharmacist who invented the drug? Do you think he just pulled that out of nowhere? He had a word from the Lord. It doesn't matter if he doesn't give God credit for it. Are you paying attention? The bottom line is, God inspired, gave wisdom, and gave knowledge to invent machines. So there are divine healings and there are physical healings, meaning healings through concoction, through diet. Who is the author and finisher of all of that? God Almighty himself.

Have you ever been healed? Have you been divinely healed? Have you had a touch from God and the sickness or the disease was gone? I have! I have medical documentation of a fatal heart condition and the side effects of it was sudden death which means no one would get to me fast enough to resuscitate me. I have a doctor's note that said I couldn't fly, I couldn't be in high elevation and I used to pass out 3 or 4 times a day. The Lord healed my body and I travel in airplanes every few weeks. I no longer pass out and I have no medications at all.

Even more exciting is the story of Kimberly, a single mom, who came to my seminar in Chicago, Illinois. The Lord had me pull her out of the audience, lay hands on her and I bound up a spirit of death, little did I know she was dying of cancer, she was completely healed that night. She went home and after a year of business failure was able to make $10,000 in 3 weeks. She led her 7 year old son to Christ. She came back to a seminar a year later and says she's cancer free, she screams out "I am still alive" and she's paid off $32,000 worth of debt in one year. Every ounce of that story is a miracle. Do you believe in that God she received a miracle from?

12) Miraculous Powers

I am going to ruffle your feathers because you may have been taught that miraculous powers don't happen today. If that's your case, that's tragic.

In my hometown I met a woman who for 38 years opens up her Bible, and in a worship service, manna comes from the Heaven and lands on her Bible. I have a piece of it in my wallet. I ate some. Tastes pretty good.

Miracles, feathers falling out of nowhere. Gold dust appearing on people's faces. We had a man who did not believe in God whose leg grew right before his wife's eyes. As you can imagine, he now believes in God. It happened. This man testified, right before his wife, tears running down his face. He said, "My leg grew." That is called a miracle.

13) Discernment Between Spirits.

The next gift is the gift of discernment. Do you have a lie-o-meter? (You know when someone is lying to you.) That is an inexperienced version of discernment. You need a better, advanced version of the gift of discernment. Distinguishing between spirits, between God and the devil, so that you know who is talking to you.

14) Speaking in Different Tongues

You may not believe in this, but the Bible talks about it. It says clearly, "Speaking in a language that you do not know, that you have not learned." All I know is people that didn't even believe in speaking in other tongues now have the gift of tongues. At a recent business seminar I was teaching at in Los Angeles, a woman by the name of Gerri told her story.

"In March of this year, it was at the end of prayer and we were standing in the back praying for people and I was behind a woman. I think I put my hands on her and I just started speaking in tongues. And I went, 'Oh my gosh. What is going on?' I just thought it was the weirdest thing I never wanted that gift. I never asked for that gift. God blessed me with that gift and I've been using it ever since. I don't know how to explain it. All I know is it happens."

He who speaks in an unknown tongue does not speak to man but speaks to God.

15) Interpretation of Tongues

The gift of interpretation is when you hear somebody

speaking in tongues and all of a sudden, you understand what they are saying and you interpret it. That's trippy.

I want you to seriously consider what I am about to say. The gifts of God are irrevocable. The Bible says, either you will use them for yourself, the enemy or for God. Which do you think will have long lasting, bearing fruit? If you use it for God, then it will have long lasting fruit. Not only that, it will be eternal instead of just temporary.

The gifts without training leads to destruction. The gift is given to us by the Spirit. The gift will be made complete by the Spirit, which means you have to spend time with the Spirit. The gift is not for your glory but His and it is for equipping the saints, a people, not a building. It's for building the Kingdom of Heaven, not just a "brick and mortar" building.

"I got my dream back, found out who I truly was and that I was wired for success!"

~ Doreen

CREATING UNITY IN A
DIVERSE CULTURE

THE ENEMY HAS a plan to divide and conquer God's people. He wants you to think that you have nothing to offer the King of Kings and the Lord of Lords. He wants to make you think that what you have is not useful for anybody else. Here are four ways that I discovered through my own experience that the enemy tries to divide and conquer:

1) **You're jealous of other people's gifts.** You're judgmental of and/or you belittle other people's gifts. You tear them apart when you do not realize that you do have a gift and you're not using it.

2) **You don't use your gifts.** Remember what we saw previously about the one who doesn't use his talent? He is considered a wicked, lazy servant. Those who receive an ability from God and do not use their gift, according to the word of God are wicked, lazy servants.

3) **If you do not know that you have a gift from God, you will abuse the gift.** You will use it for the wrong reasons. You will use it to glorify yourself instead of God, and you will exalt yourself

instead of exalting God and others.

4) You feel useless and worthless. You feel that your life is a waste of time and that you are isolated and alone.

You should know by now that you are being used by God, even when you don't know it. What a loving God. We're going to work together, not put each other down. We're not going to try to change each other. We're all different parts of one body. We can't survive without each other's gifts. It's time that we recognize our gifts, use them to the fullest, accept other people's gifts, embrace their gifts and then cheer them on. Go!

What we have done is put walls in the body of Christ. You see, the Bible says the body of Christ is us. We represent the body. The body of Christ, the church, is not a building with walls. It is wall-less. And for those of us that are in Christ, we represent Christ and we are the church. That's who we are. You may be reading this and like me were taught in good-heartedness but ignorance that those gifts are a result of super-duper spiritual people only in the right church.

Now, I ask you, who in the world would want you to believe that you are not special and that you cannot use all your gifts? Tell me, who would want you to think that you have no access to miraculous powers? Who would want you to believe that you have no access to the spirit of prophecy? Who would want you to believe that you do not have access to healing? Who would want you to believe that you do not have access to tongues, and interpretation of tongues? Who would want you not to believe that you don't have access to wisdom and knowledge? Who? The destroyer. Yea, the stupid, ugly, sick and disgusting, devil who was defeated 2,000 years ago, who has a big, fat, nasty, sick, and disgusting mouth.

Here's the truth. If he can get you to believe you don't have access to the gifts of the spirit, you certainly won't use them now, will you? And if you don't use them, you're certainly not a threat to the kingdom of darkness, now are you?

Now, let's see what Ephesians 4, verse 11, says. "It was He who gave some to be apostles, some to be prophets, some to be evangelists, and some to be pastors and teachers, to prepare God's people for works of service so that the body of Christ may be built up until we reach unity in the faith and in the knowledge of the Son of God, and become mature attaining to the whole measure of the fullness of Christ."

In the last chapter, we defined every single one of the gifts of the Spirit. What we didn't do is define the positions: evangelist, pastor, teacher, apostle, and prophet. We're going to define those in this next section, and the point of the message is to show you how to create unity in a diverse culture.

Apostles

Ephesians 4:11 says "It was He who gave some to be apostles." Let's talk about what that looks like. I'm going to tell you what that means in layman terms. The text doesn't say evangelists in the church, apostles in seminary, or prophets in a four walled building. It does not say that. There are no walls, no boundaries at all. But somehow, we have decided that those titles are only set for those in 'traditional ministry'.

Let me prove something to you. David was the apple of God's eye and he was not a pastor. Did you know that David didn't go to seminary? He was a warrior! The apple of God's eye was a warrior, a worshiper, and a king.

Did you know that John the Baptist was not a traditional minister? He didn't go to seminary to learn how to baptize or preach? Anyone of us that are in Christ can baptize another. That's the truth. You see, somehow, we have created these rules and regulations which do not exist in the Bible.

What is an apostle according to scriptures? An apostle is the head of an organization. This can be someone who is a forerunner who starts something out of thin air, a leader who equips other leaders to lead. An apostle can also operate as an evangelist, prophet, pastor and teacher with signs and wonders following.

They can pastor, which means that they can nourish the people that are following them. They can feed them and protect them, and help to groom them. It means that they can teach, which means that they can equip other people with new skills that they did not have prior to meeting them. Signs and wonders, according to the Bible, follow an apostle.

So, a founder of a company, a forerunner, somebody that has a vision, tests the vision, collaborates and brings people along to dig those trenches and get out there and make a way to make it happen. Almost even like a general contractor. Have you ever met a general contractor? Are you yourself a general contractor? That's an apostolic anointing. A contractor is somebody that can actually do all parts of that job. He sees a plot of dirt and says, "I see a building." He formulates the plans, hires the people, and pulls them all together to get the job done.

According to the Bible, that's an apostle. Somebody who is pretty much a fire starter, goes in, digs in the trench, starts with nothing, builds something, moves on to something else, and leaves those people fully trained and able to handle everything without them. That's an apostolic anointing.

Prophets

These are futuristic thinkers, they're doers, people that are speaking visions, speaking about the future, speaking where we're going to be some day. Do you know people like this? That's a prophetic gift. They're the ones who cast visions. They bring a fresh message, often they bring correction. They'll call you on your stuff. They also bring you to restoration. Have you ever studied the Bible? It's so good, you gotta read the whole thing.

If you study the prophets in the Bible, Micah is a prime example. He was a prophet and during his time the priests were doing wrong. The king was doing wrong. And he was some no-name, nobody from nowhere, with nothing, who went up to the governmental authorities and said, "God is going to get you. You are taking bribes from the rich and you are not giving justice to the poor." That's what he said. "You are not doing things right, and if you do not repent and turn away from your wicked ways, God is going to spank you!"

He went to the king and said, "If you do not turn from your wicked ways, if you don't honor God, and you do not worship Him in the high places, then He is going to spank you ugly!" That's Micah. The desire of a prophet is to bring people to restoration and reconciliation.

Is that you? Do you know people who are like that? They're not titled prophetess or prophet on their business card at such and such assemblies or whatever, church. Many have the gift and don't know it because of the boundaries that we put on the gift and the calling.

Evangelists

This is somebody that likes to get things done, now. They are results oriented. Not next year, not next week, but now. They are always great promoters, always have people around them. Great recruiters, great in sales, always making a flurry of things happen, out of absolutely nowhere. They create chaos out of thin air. This is obviously a person who's called into ministry. The evangelist comes out in winning souls for the Kingdom of Heaven. That's how that's exemplified, but the same exact gifts operate in those that are selling something. They want to promote, want to rally. They're motivators. Do you know people like this? They have the gift of evangelism, they just don't know it.

Pastors

Pastors are the ones that want to shepherd people. They have a flock; they have people that follow them. They want to nurture and protect. Someone in management sometimes can be a pastor. The heart of a pastor is the heart of somebody wanting to create a safe place, they want to huddle, and love on you. That's the way they are. You go to their house and they bring you a cup of tea and rub your back.

Teachers

Finally, we have teachers. A teacher is someone who has a very important job. God does not necessarily hold one higher than the other. A teacher's job is to equip the next generation. They show vital things that have to be done. Without teachers, folks, none of us would know how to read, write, add, subtract. That is the position of a teacher. They pass on knowledge and wisdom. The Bible says that My people perish for a lack of knowledge. They are passing down to the next group tradition, wisdom, knowledge, so that they can carry it through the next generation following that.

Do you qualify in any of those five positions? Of course, all of us do. The unfortunate thing is that most people in those positions have not been trained in how to deal with people, which is what their entire life and career is centered around. This is where and why we have so many people wounded and walking away from God. This is so important which is why I said in the last chapter; "Gifting without training leads to destruction."

Operating in Unity

My point with all this is that it is evident that we all have different functions. We all have different gifts. We all have different abilities, and with all those differences, we carry different places where we've come from. We are coming from a different state of mind, a different point of view. This is why arguing happens, because we all have our own personal points of view and our personal agenda on what we passionately feel is the right way to do things.

So, with unity there is something important to understand about people's gifts and to explode with those gifts. However, in most cases people are stunting the gifts of others. They are stunting people's growth, which is neither fair, nor right.

So, because of all the different points of view that we have, because of all the different opinions that we have, I want you to imagine for a minute, the illustration of the United States Military. There are different branches that specialize in different functions. We have the Navy, Air Force, Army and Marines. The Navy watches over the water, while the Air Force protects the skies, and the Marines are security. So, if you imagine the different branches of the military, all of them have specific trained knowledge in specific areas. Well, all of them have gifts by the same, one and the same Spirit.

So, we know that anything divided against itself will not

stand. This is where we need a very large level of maturity, to understand that everybody has different gifts. The key is, in business and any leadership role (ministry, family, etc.), to give a platform for those gifts to be able to be exemplified.

Leaders must make room for those gifts to be able to be groomed, edified, and provide a place where they can come out, instead of being stuck in a cubicle, so to speak.

Here are three things that make it is impossible to have unity.

1) It's impossible to have unity with jealousy. It is absolutely impossible to have unity in an organization when there is jealousy present. Jealousy of people's gifts, recognition, position, money, their wife (or husband), or of their happiness. If there is jealousy in the organization, there will not be unity. Jealousy causes division.

2) Judgments. It is impossible to have unity with judgment. Judgment that belittles somebody's gifts, position, or success; and non acceptance of certain people, causes division, not unity. When you won't listen, you're critical and you have to be the chief authority on everything that is absolute judgment. You're exalting yourself.

3) Pride. It's impossible to have unity where there is pride. Pride being everything is set up to serve you. You must have the credit for everything even for things that you didn't do. You have to do everything yourself. "Nobody else can do it better than me, so I'm the chief authority, just sit down and shut up. I'll take care of all 25 of those things tomorrow." Pride showing up in that you think it's your job to change people. The only one you can change is who? You, and how you deal with the inadequacies in other people. How you deal with incompetence.

Now, let me show you what the glue is for unity.

Love

These are not necessarily in any particular order, but number one is love. It is impossible to have unity in your marriage, family, business, etc., without love. I'm talking about love for the head or leader. So, for example, for me and my life, the head is my God and my husband. The head inside of our corporation is Hans.

Love in the second area, is for one another—a brotherly love, a three-fold cord that can't be easily broken. A love where you will cover each other, and honor one another. The third is the love for the vision of what the organization represents and what it stands for.

So, you need love for your leader, you need love for one another, and you need love for the vision. You're looking for people that will love your vision and love the game. Have you ever noticed watching the Olympics, that those athletes love their game? It's powerful. That's what you're looking for in your family, ministry and business, my friend. People that are going to love the game and love the vision. You're eventually going to teach them how to love the head.

Acceptance

The glue in the unity is acceptance. Acceptance exemplified in this way—mercy. Being merciful to one another, for one another, in times of trials, and with mistakes. You have to make a decision. If you want a unified organization, if you want a unified family, then you will be one of those people that cover each other's backs, instead of kicking people when they're down. Instead of reminding them of their mistakes, you remind them of their position that they're called to, you remind them that you believe in them, that you show mercy even when it doesn't make any sense.

Here's what I know. In Chronicles, it says, "He is rich in mercy, slow to anger, gracious and compassionate." All you have to do is read the Bible and you will see that this is true. He should have killed His own people a thousand times. And if it were me, I would have, wouldn't you? Four hundred years of total defilement. I mean, come on God, spank 'em already. That's me, I'm human.

a) Acceptance is covering each other's backs.

b) Acceptance is to receive and embrace each other's gifts, not trying to change their gifts to be like yours. Acceptance in an organization is so powerful, so huge. Before now, were you not in an organization that showed these three different areas of acceptance? Was it a safe place to grow in? Have you now encountered a safe place to grow in where there is merciful acceptance to cover your back? The kind of acceptance to say, "I love your gifts. Let's find a place that we can use it because I believe in your future."

Would you agree that would just be the most powerful place to be involved with? Then create the place, I did with my companies. Create acceptance in your environment, and you will be amazed at the kind of production that you will see.

Teamwork

Teamwork is the opportunity for each to use their gifts for the benefit of the whole. Oftentimes leaders have a very big challenge with teamwork. A lot of leaders are single players. I will tell you that you cannot build what's in your heart by yourself. You cannot, you will not, you will crack. I'm going to tell you—I don't care how great you think you are, you are not going to get to the top by yourself. It's just not going to happen. You're going to get to the top with the help of others' gifts that are better than yours, no question.

Humility

Humility is also glue in unity. Thinking of others higher than yourself. I have heard that preached so wrong it's pathetic. Thinking others higher than yourself is not putting yourself down. Thinking others higher than yourself doesn't mean that you squash yourself to make them feel better. To be honest with you, that's called false humility.

Humility is when you know you're nothing without God. You know only He can satisfy. You know you only have because He has given. Essentially, humility is a condition of the heart, false humility is pride.

Encouragement

Encouragement is huge glue in the area of unity. Encouragement, number one, is what eggs people on; be their biggest fan. You egg people on to be the best they're called to be. Believe in them even when they don't believe in themselves. You encourage them to step beyond where they think is possible, beyond what they think that they can do, beyond anything that they have ever done, and you're the biggest cheerleader saying, "I know you can, and I know it's possible because of the God that dwells within."

Have you ever been around an organization that encourages you like that? What has happened to you in that environment? Did you soar? Do you think that would make an incredibly powerful organization, one that would be unstoppable? Well step up and learn how to create one.

Honor

It's impossible to have unity without honor. Earlier I mentioned the military, in our branches of the military, there is respect for the chain of command and honor for every single one of those positions. They are taught honor in boot camp. It is evident to me that people don't know how to honor as it rarely ever happens.

Honor is extremely important and it's part of the glue that exists in our organization. I'm going to tell you what that looks like in the Bible and there's been some myths taught on that, which is really sad. God thinks honor is pretty important. Honor is mentioned 147 times in the Bible. And I'm going to show you some places that might shock you. Barak asked a woman to go with him into battle. Because he was chicken for the moment, he came under the spirit of stupid. He forgot who his God was for a moment. So, Deborah in Judges 4:9 said, "Very well, I will go with you. But, because of the way you're going about this, the honor will not be yours, for the Lord will hand Sisera over to a woman." She tells him that he will not get the honor because he has not stepped up to his rightful position. The honor will be mine, buddy. I will defeat our enemy (and she did). There's Deborah in her stilettos, walking through dirt, all dolled up and her hair teased and combed back, with her highlights, going, "Hey, sucker, step up, buddy, or the honor is mine." That one story, for some reason, isn't talked about very much.

We've been told, somehow in the church that you're not supposed to be honored. Please read the 147 texts that talk about honor. In fact, let me just nullify that little lie right now in your head. Have you heard that you're not supposed to honor each other? That defiles about 200 other scriptures. It's a lie. That is a man who's afraid of people walking in pride. They're still walking in pride because they're walking in false humility.

Deuteronomy 26:19 will shock your socks off. "He has declared that He will set you in praise, fame, and honor high above all the nations." You!

1 Samuel 2:30 says, "Those who honor Me, I will honor, but those who despise Me will be disdained," which means scorned, despised. So, God is saying, "If you honor Me, I will honor you." Honor's pretty important to Him, and honor is very important to people. We see honor in the Bible in the form of coats, sashes, and crowns. We see that Joseph was given a coat of honor. It's being set apart, that's what it is. You need to understand that chain of command that exists in organizations and edify that leader.

The other thing is that you need to honor one another. The Bible says to honor your father and mother. Have you heard this? We're to honor each other. What does that look like? What does that mean?

The Bible is clear, because God honored His people. He put a coat of honor over Joseph, others were given a crown of honor, still others a sash of honor. The Bible shows us that there were certain tunics of honor, people were honored with food, or gifts. We live in a nation today that has very little honor. Many of us go to churches that have no honor. Our youth today do not know the meaning of honor. Honor is giving credit where credit is due. You can't steal from somebody's influence and call it your own.

We have a society of people that are just raping and pillaging each other, of honor. Honor is being able to verbalize and talk about someone as seen through God's eyes. So often we're afraid to edify one another. We don't want them to get a "big head," so therefore we don't honor.

Honoring one another is honoring God, my friend. God speaks through others. When you honor who He spoke through, you honor Him. Just like it says in the Bible, if you honor your father and mother, you're honoring God. Do you want to know what it means to honor your mother and father? I got set free for this one. You bring honor to your father's house by how you conduct yourself in your own house. You bring honor to your mother by how you treat others. You are honoring.

What does honor look like? Honor is respect. Honor is dignity that you give to other people and you allow them to be who they are and to share their story. Recognizing someone who helped you get someplace that you could not get on your own.

Honor can really even be as simple as a card. Honor can be something as simple as recognizing somebody's strengths. Honor could also be recognizing someone that's going through a hard time. Just a simple touch on the shoulder saying, "You know what? I know things are kind of difficult for you right now, but I'm praying for you." That's honor. Honor is uplifting, it's edifying, it's encouraging, that's what it is and it's impossible to have unity without honor.

Interrupting people is dishonoring. Being argumentative is dishonor. No support is dishonor. Expecting something for nothing is dishonor. Expecting somebody to do what you're not willing to do for them is dishonor. A one-way deal is dishonor. I think the best way to look at it is just look at the military and how they are set up. You wouldn't think about not saluting properly. Whether you agreed with the orders or not, you had to honor, and you had to support the head.

Obedience

The final point is obedience. Again, if you were in the military, you know what obedience is all about. Regardless if you agree, you know that you need to obey. There are four different types of obedience. Really, there's only one obedience and the other ones are sort of trying to be obedient.

The first one is reluctant obedience. Reluctant obedience is when you have to be pushed to do something. Have you ever met someone like that? Yet we can't figure out why we can't succeed or why your business isn't blessed. There's this reluctance in you that says something like, "I don't know. I'm just not sure." That's reluctance. Just like I tell my children, I'm going to tell you, there's no blessing with reluctant obedience. In fact, reluctant obedience is a curse that you receive instantaneously.

The second form is a grudging obedience. "Fine! I'll do it! I don't wanna and I don't like it." If you have children, have you seen them do something like this? That is rebellion, not obedience, and it comes with a curse. Reluctant obedience and grudging obedience cause stress in your life. It causes the destiny to be prolonged. It causes hardship, headaches and division; that's the fulfillment of the curse.

The third one is a willing obedience. The only reason I can talk about these four levels of obedience is because I have experienced them firsthand. I was the worst with obedience! Willing was like a curse word, I would only obey as a martyr. When my husband would take a stand on something he felt strong about, I would say, "Ok fine! I'll do it" but inside I'm saying, "NOOOOO!" Until the Lord convicted me while I was disciplining my son (who was told to do something and was not willingly obeying), as the words were flying out of my mouth. I quickly ran to my bathroom and cried because I was completely guilty of the same thing! I would obey but I'd obey unwillingly and with a grudge—that does NOT get a blessing. There's a blessing that comes with being willing to obey.

The final and fourth form of obedience is a fully abandoned, fully surrendered obedience. You see, with the willing obedience that I had experienced, there was still fear and no guarantee, but I was just going to trust. I still was afraid to be willingly obedient. I would do it. I pushed down the grudge, pushed away the reluctance, and I was willing to obey, still afraid, still not fully trusting. But then you come to a place where there is a fully abandoned, fully surrendered obedience with no guarantee at all of any result. This is what Christ exemplified on the cross, a fully surrendered obedience for your life and mine.

There is a great blessing and it honors God for us to fully surrender with full on abandonment, with absolutely no guarantee. Do you need to get there? Can you see between all the things that I mentioned, love, honor, and obedience, why there hasn't been unity in what you're doing?

It's impossible to have unity without fully abandoned, surrendered obedience. The Lord has been telling you what you're supposed to do. He's been loud and clear with confirmation, with great signs and wonders. He wants you to obey.

My daughter, when she was in the fifth grade, kept asking me to home school her. I said "I can't do that. I wasn't smart in school. I teach adults how to succeed. I cannot teach reading, writing, and arithmetic," but I kept hearing, "home school Arika," and Arika kept begging me. The cry of her heart was to get out of the school and be home to learn with me.

I was reading my Bible one day and I came upon Moses and Noah, and I had this huge revelation, enormous revelation and the revelation was that God spoke details to His people. Look at the details that Noah received from God. If he missed one little centimeter of a detail, none of us would be alive today. However, he heard the details and he obeyed.

CHAPTER FIVE

I read about Moses and him getting all the laws and all of the strategic things that they were supposed to do. I jumped out of bed on the floor, and I lay prostrate before the Lord, and I said, "God, I want to hear You like that. I want to hear those details. I want You to tell me what to eat for lunch! I want to hear every little detail." I heard an audible voice say to me, "I do. You just don't listen!" After balling my eyes out I got up and went to church and I hear a voice, during worship, "Home school Arika" and I said, "I rebuke you, Satan, in the name of Jesus."

God is my witness. I said, "I rebuke you, in Jesus' name" and He said, "This is Jesus, and you will trust Me, and you will home school Arika." How gracious and compassionate He is.

For almost a year He had been speaking this to me and I just didn't listen. I didn't know it was His voice. Actually I didn't want to hear that answer, I just pretended that I did. So I ignored it. Have you ever done that? It's the same as when a child asks the mother for a piece of candy and she says no, so he goes and asks the father, wanting a different answer.

By the way, home schooling turned out to be an amazing experience and something I will always treasure. She's been on several missions trips, recorded a CD, had time to develop her musical talents, all are things that wouldn't have happened if she were still in private school. I'm so grateful God "made" me do it.

Do you know that He has been directing you, answering certain things for you, putting you in places, and confirming what He's telling you to do? Have you chosen not to hear? It's impossible to receive a blessing unless you obey—fully surrendered obedience

"I believe these are the core issues that keep people from getting results in their life. These issues must be dealt with... Dani is under the anointing, no question about it. I cannot get enough of the Bible scriptures to help me 'conquer the financial Kingdom'. My 'financial blueprint' is changing. Thank you Dani for a 'no-fluff' agenda. No sugar-coating here. TRUTH ROCKS!"

~ Allison V.

WHAT KIND OF SERVANT ARE YOU?

I WAS SITTING IN church and my pastor mentioned that the week before he had spoken about the Parable of the Talents. I sank in my chair because I was thinking, "Lord you've given me much and what have I done with it. At that point I had been retired for several years and thought I would never speak again and I was no longer equipping people to succeed in the marketplace—I was at home being a mom.

A great conviction came over me and I repented. I went home, laid on the floor and I said, "Lord, God forgive me. You've given me much and I'm doing nothing with it." So, I want you to discover which of the three servants you are, and how you get promoted out of the position that you're in right now. Do you want to be promoted?

God is Your Publicist

The first thing you need to realize is that God is The Promoter. You need to learn how to make yourself so valuable that your company, organization, whatever you want promotion with will do anything to keep you. Don't worry that your boss doesn't see what you do. God will remind the right people at the right time, at the right place who has put in the work, who is committed, who's had a good attitude, and will make a way where there is no way for you to be the one ushered in to get that promotion. But you have to do your part and that's what you're about to learn.

Next, you'll want to understand that the marketplace pays for value, not for your need. The only thing that will determine your value in the marketplace is your skill. So don't bring your need to the marketplace—you'll starve—bring your skill!

My personal belief is that if we are a chosen generation for Him, if we are a child of the Most High God and it's time for a promotion, who should get it?

Example: There's a management position in a company and two people are going for it. One is a Christian and one is not. The Christian is doing what he's been taught to do, pray, ask God to open the door for you and then sit and watch a favorite rerun. A non-Christian is increasing his skills by taking a few extra classes and learning from the right people to qualify for the position. So you tell me, who gets the job? The answer is obvious and will be scripturally revealed through this chapter.

Here's a reality check. Most of us are sitting around—not you, of course—saying "What's on TV? Or let's buy a lottery ticket." Total poverty mindset. Faith is action. It is not sitting around saying, "Oh, Lord, pay off our debt!", "Get us in a different neighborhood!", "Find me a new job!" God is saying, "Shut up already and go to work!" It says that. Not in those exact words, but it says that in the Bible.

I believe Christians are supposed to prosper, but what are you doing to make that happen? Are you sitting around waiting for God to bless you when you need something? How do you think it's supposed to work? Do you think that all of a sudden God just rips you out of the house you're in and drops another one on top of you? You think you're going to win the lottery? Get lucky in Vegas?

I know this: the harder you work as unto Him, the more you get blessed. That's what I know. Most people don't do that.

I have several points to share with you about promotion.

1. God is Your Promoter

He sees what you do and He also sees what you don't do. He knows when you're naughty and nice. This is the truth my friend. He sees if you're doing it with the spirit of excellence. He sees if you're doing it diligently. He sees who you're doing it for. If it's all about you and your recognition then it's all in vain. Work as unto Him, knowing that He's right there beside you every single day, all the time going, "Yes! Go! You can do it. Keep going."

2. You are the Owner of Ability

Remember the Parable of the Talents (Matthew 25:14-26)? Everyone has a talent. All three servants got something. It says, "He gave each one according to their own ability." All of them got something, all of them got a gift from God, "according to their ability." What does that say to you and me?

Have you ever raised your ability? Can you remember when you started off on your job years and years ago? Remember when your abilities stunk? With time, training and trial and error, what happened to your ability? It got better and you then mastered the task. Did your confidence grow? It said that the master came and gave according to their ability. Who is in charge of the ability department? You. "But Dani, I'm lacking in the ability department." What are you going to do about it? Give up? Give in?

What do you do if you don't have an ability? Go get yourself trained and equipped. "I don't know business." So what! Go learn.

Do you know you can learn to do anything? Isn't that awesome? We are co-laborers with Christ. What does that mean? He carries his 50 bricks you carry yours. Together, you get the entire load carried. That's what that means.

Do you have some abilities that you are using? The more you use those abilities, the better they become.

The more you invest into those skills, the better they become.

3. Can you pass the Test?

Point number three is, he leaves. This is amazing to me. He leaves and he comes back a long time later. Why did he give them the talent and then leave? He wanted to see what they were going to do with them. He's thinking, "Okay. Well, I got three people. I'm putting out this challenge and I'll see who is going to step up." We've done this in companies for years. I'll put a challenge out there, and then see who steps up. That's what he did. He gave out the three talents. He wanted to see who was going to step up. He did not hover over the three.

In the codependent society that we live in, he left. Many of us are hovering over our children in case they make a mistake. It says he left, he let them step up on their own to do what they were going to do. He gave them the gift and then he left to see what they would do with it.

4. Honoring the Opportunity

Let's talk about the first servant who was given five talents. You know what I think he did? This is the 'Dani version' of the Parable of Talents. It said that he left at once and invested the money, and what did he do? He doubled the money. He took the five talents that his master had given him and he says, "Okay. I think I better find a business. So the first servant, he goes out and he invests in a business. He made an investment and he doubled his money. So now he doesn't have five but has doubled his money and now has ten.

Let me tell you what the first servant didn't do. He did not say, "That master, he's just always giving me this load of work to do and then he leaves. I don't want my boss to get any more credit for my success. I don't want this company to prosper anymore from my efforts. Forget it. I am not doing anything." I know Christians and non-Christians that do that, and expect to get blessed.

You can't sow that seed. "I'm not going to help. They haven't helped me. What have they done for me? There ain't no way I can move up anyway. This whole thing is a bottleneck. All the people are already at the top and I'm just the bottom feeder."

That is not what that first servant did. He was so grateful for the opportunity to go out there and do something, because he was given a chance. You've been given a chance to succeed as well.

5. Spirit of Excellence

It says that he did it immediately. The servant did it with a spirit of excellence. He did it diligently. That's what he went and did. He wasn't focused on anything else besides, "I'm going to make my master proud."

6. Trust Your Master

Here's another thing the first servant did. He trusted his master's character. "You know what? I'm right here right now. I better make the best of it." Can you say honestly that you have not quite given your business, your marriage, etc... the spirit of excellence that you know you should? Part of that is because you really have not quite had the revelation about the God you serve. You seem to think you've found this little life all by your-self. All of this was by the hand of God. It says, "He moves the heavens and the earth to make His will come to pass." What are the odds of you reading this book? Have you been searching for ways to improve your life? Have you been working hard and hit-ting a brick wall, looking for answers as to why? Ask and you shall receive.

7. Lessons from Servant Number Two

Let's talk about servant number two. He did the same thing. He went out immediately and he doubled his profits. He had two talents. He invested two talents, and boom, he wound up prosper-ing. Let me tell you what servant number two did not do. He didn't whine about only receiving two talents. He did not say, "You know what? You got five, and I only got two? I always get the short end of the stick." I never get to win. Hasn't that happened to you before? He didn't do that. He didn't call his friend Ezekiel and say, "Ezekiel. I was with my master today and he is such a jerk. He gave Shakeem five tal-ents, and I got gypped again and I only got two." He didn't do that.

He wasn't ungrateful to that high position, he did not compare. He did not compare what he got to what somebody else got. He did not make a comparison and say, "Well forget it then. When I get five, then I'll make it double and I'll do good. When I get to that director position, then I'll give it my best shot." "When I get that management position, boy I'm telling you what. Watch out, because I'm really going to shine then."

You have to shine first before you get the position. You have to shine first before you get the promotion. You have to be trusted first with what you have before you ever think about rising up be-yond where you're at. That's the only way that it works. He did not say, "That does it. I'm never going to be good enough anyway, so why even try?   Nothing ever works out for me anyway. Everyone always winds up getting promoted ahead of me. This is always where I wind up, second best all the time. So what's the point?" I know you're not like this, but I am sure you know somebody like this. Servant number two knew who the promoter was so he went out and he gave it his best shot; with the spirit of excellence, with diligence, not looking to the right or to the left. Not looking at who was watching him. Not looking at what somebody else got or didn't get. With a total spirit of gratefulness, with the complete spirit of excellence and diligence, he went out and took care of what he was given. The master came back and doubled the blessing. That's how you get promoted.

8. Delusional Servant Number Three

Let's look at my favorite servant, number three. Number three was given a talent, and what did he do with it? Do you remember? He dug a hole and he buried it. I have to confess to you, that was me, not too long ago. I buried my talents and I said I would never speak again, never to raise up others to succeed again. I even sold the clothes I designed that I used to wear on stage. I sold everything and settled in my lot as a Christian woman to serve as a mother and wife, and that's it. There was nothing else for me.

The role of mother and wife is a powerful role. I'm still doing it. At my house, everyday when my kids get out of school, I'm with my kids. I travel once a month. I home school. I'm a cooking freak. I still do laundry. I still do dishes. You can ask any one who knows me. I'm still a mom and a wife. That is my powerful role.

Here's another very interesting thing. It says he dug a hole and buried it, and it says, "And he hid the Lord's money." Did you catch that? Whose money is in your pocket, your bank? He has entrusted you with an amount. Are you taking care of it, and are you investing it wisely, or are you blowing it? Good question.

It says the Lord's money, the Lord's talent, the Lord's gift. It says that he buried the Lord's money. All that you have is His, and when you can come to that revelation, you will treat things so much more differently. All that you are is His. He knitted you together in your mother's womb. He set a plan for you before the beginning of the foundations of the world. What are you doing with the talents that He has given you? You were born with gifts, you were born with talents. The Bible says there's not one person that was born without them. We were all born with something. It is His.

What are you doing with it? Are you using it? Do you know that you have a gift or a talent? Would you say that you need a little bit of work in the area of using it? Doing something with it? Why do you think the third servant hid that talent? It says in the Bible, "I hid the talent because I was afraid."

What was he afraid of—failure, rejection? Why aren't you using your talents? It's a question to ask yourself. Do you think that they're not good enough?

Let's go back to Matthew 25:24 "Then the man who had received one talent says, 'Master, I know that you are a hard man, harvesting where you have not sown, gathering where you have not scattered seed. So I was afraid and went out and hid your talent in the ground. See? Here you have what belongs to you.'"

Don't you think it's a little strange that the other two did not feel the same way about the master? So what I believe happened is that the servant who was given the one talent was absolutely ungrateful for what he was given. He probably looked at the other two and said, "How come I didn't get that?" He probably was one of those that said, "That wicked master that I serve. I work so hard, and yet

I never get a piece of the action." Or he could have been afraid of disappointing his master and had a confidence issue. He had excuses that left his talent dormant.

This was a servant who was delusional. There were three servants. Two of the servants with the spirit of gratefulness and excellence, and diligence went out to please their master. But here's the one servant who had a judgment against the master and said, "You're a hard man, and I was afraid. So here, you can have what is yours." Isn't that the wildest thing? Why is it that the third one had a completely different point of view than the other two?

Do you have a prejudgment on God in a very similar way; that you think no matter how hard you work, no matter how hard you try, that it's not going to work for you anyway. That's what the third servant thought. He believed that his master was a wicked man. He did not know the character of his master. Do you know the character of your master? Because if you really truly knew the character of your master, you would go at it with everything you've got. Fear would not fit into the equation. Fear of failure, fear of rejection, fear of man, would not fit into the equation if you really knew the character of your master.

The first two knew the character of their master, and they knew, "I'm going to make him proud, and he will bless me." The last one did not know the character of his master and, therefore, did a wicked thing.

9. Tested for Promotion

All three servants were being tested for a promotion. Two took a risk and made an increase. The third servant didn't past the test.

My heart hurts when I see my brothers and sisters not being

all that they can be. My heart pains when I see people putting hindrances in their life when they serve such a glorious God, who wants them to succeed, who wants them to shine. He wants for the world to see, "Look what I've done with my son. Look what I've done with my daughter. That's my workmanship."

He will put you on platforms and give you a chance. Do you know your Master? Do you know you've been given a talent, a gift from God?

Have you Rejected Your Gift or Talent?

You may have a gift to sing and you're not using it and you're thinking, "Well it's not good enough." Step out in faith and believe that it is His spirit on your tongue that makes it good enough, that He can make a way where there is no way. When the church won't let a woman in to speak because of the way she looks. "Ooh, you're too curvy. You need to cut your hair and don't wear any makeup." I almost did. I'm not kidding you. The last time the head of a women's ministry said to me, "You know, Dani, the women have a hard time with your long flowing hair and you're a little busty." Did I ask for this?

When you were doing womb service, did you order the size of your nose? Me neither. You know, when you were doing womb service, did you ask for your waistline, the color of your eyes, the color of your skin? None of us did. I went home after hearing this message from this woman and I said, "Okay, God. Do you want me to change all that I am? Do you want me to cut my hair off and not wear any makeup?"

I started praying about it, and I cried. I said, "Lord, do You want me to do these things?" I said, "Take my boldness away, God." For five years, I asked my God, my Creator of the Heavens and the

Earth, to take the gift that He gave me, which was boldness. "Take away my boldness, God." Why? Because it offended Christians. This is what He said. He said, "I gave you that boldness, and you will use it for My glory. I gave you that hair, and you will use it for My glory. I gave you that body, and you will use it for My glory." This is what He said. "Just as Esther was trained up for such a time as her time, I have trained you up for such a time as this. You be who I created you to be, and you conform to the image of Christ, and not to the image of man." For some reason that scripture has been twisted to lead us to believe that conforming to other Christian opinion is OK—NOT—it says to the image of Christ—not man who is trying to BE Christ.

Do You Know Your God?

Do you know the character of your God, or have you believed some pulpit somewhere that said, "Meekness is poverty." That's a lie and it doesn't say that anywhere in the Bible. Have you believed that you are not supposed to succeed?

Is it All About You?

Here's another one. Have you been given a gift and you use the gift for your own glory and recognition? That was me for a lot of years. I used my gifts for my fame, and it was wrong. I'm telling you, it was empty. The Bible says that whatever you do to gain recognition from man, you have already received your reward in full, and there ain't nothing for you after that.

Do not seek your own glory because it is not as rewarding as you think. I know a whole lot of people that are so empty inside. Do you want fame and fortune and to be totally miserable? Do you want to be humble and set a good example with those riches and fame? Are you using your gifts or your talent for God's glory?

Have You Hidden Your Gift Because of Fear of Man?

Have you hidden your gift and talent because of rejection of man? Have you hidden it because of the fear of man? Oh, please, He's going to hunt you down for the rest of your life. You might as well give in now. I'm serious. The Bible says, "Many are called but few are chosen." You were chosen to do something great. So with your gift and talent, have you hidden it because of doubt? Have you hidden it because you doubt that it's going to work? Have you taken a risk on your talent that you've been given, or do you feel it's not important anyway? Have you belittled the gift or talent that God gave you? "It's nothing. It's no big deal." You do beautiful art; "Oh, that's nothing. It's no big deal. I can't do anything with it anyway."

Do you have a gift with numbers, and you belittle it? Do you compare it to somebody else's? Let me tell you something. Whatever your gift is, He wants you to grow it. He gave you your smarts. If you've got a great brain, He gave it to you because He wants you to prosper it. If you have a gift in business, He gave it to you because He wants you to double it. If you have a gift with people, He gave it to you because He wants you to prosper it.

Whatever it is that you have, whatever gift and talent that you have, He gave it to you. Do not belittle that gift because that's what the third servant did.

How do I have proof that the third servant belittled the gift? He dug a hole and buried it. If that isn't belittling I don't know what is. Have you from time to time dug a hole and buried your gift?

The last part of this scripture says, "He came to settle accounts with them." He came to settle accounts with each one of these servants. Let's go through and see what it says. Verse 20 and 21 says, to the first servant "Well done good and faithful servant. You were faithful over a few things, I will make you ruler over many things. Enter into the joy of your Lord." He also let them keep their talents.

So here he gave them a talent, let them go invest it, they doubled the profit and he gave it to them. The same with the second servant. The second servant came to him, and said, "Lord, here is your talent plus two more." They brought their profits to the Lord. You mean they didn't keep them? They didn't spend them? They brought them back to the master and said, "Here you go," and the master said what? "Keep it. It's all yours."

Both servants said that. This tells me that our God is fair. He gave all of them a gift. He is more than fair, is He not? Have you believed from time to time that God is not fair? I have felt the same way.

When you see a car crash and you see a mom and a baby die, you're like, "That's not fair." But we don't know all the circumstances that were involved, and we also don't know the outcome of the big picture of things. I know this, my God is fair. He is over-fair. He not only gave them the money to get started, but he let them keep the bounty from it.

The guy with the five and the guy with the two, He let both of them keep their doubling. He didn't say, "Well listen, little guy, I don't think you're ready to keep the profits, so why don't you go try again?" No, he said, "Keep it." To both of them he said, "Good job. Well done, good and faithful servant. Come and share in your master's inheritance."

Let's get to my favorite one, verse 24. To the man who had received one talent, the master replied, "You wicked, lazy servant." Have you ever heard of the scripture that says, "The wealth of the wicked will be transferred to the righteous"?

Let's look again at Verse 24, "His master replied, You wicked lazy servant." When you think of wickedness, you think of murder, you think of pornography, right? What does Verse 24 tell us? That laziness in God's eyes is wickedness. Not using your talent is wicked. Not doubling the profits is wicked. Don't take it up with me. I didn't write it. That's what it says. Now don't you think that's weird? This scripture is talking about money, and God is calling the servant, who buried the talent, a wicked servant, and the wealth of the wicked will be transferred to the righteous. So does that mean that if you do not use your talent, if you do not go to work, if you do not prosper with what you've been given, if you do not prosper where you're planted, you are considered wicked? That's what it says. Wow. Let's keep going.

"So you knew that I harvest where I have not sown, and gather where I have not scattered seed. Well then, you should have put your money on deposit with the bankers, so that when I returned I would have received it back with interest."

Watch this. "Take the talent from him and give it to the one who has ten talents, for everyone who has will be given more, and he will have an abundance. Whoever does not have, even what he has will be taken from him, and throw that worthless servant outside into darkness, where there will be weeping and gnashing of teeth." This is clearly stating that if you are not using your talents, your gifts that God has given you, that is wicked.

Do you like getting spanked by God? Me neither. He says, "For everyone who has will be given more. He who does not have even what he already has will be taken from him." God cherishes hard workers. He blesses those who work diligently with the spirit of excellence. Do you want a promotion? Then you better start investing your talent. Start using your gifts without fear, without hesitation, without confusion, without all this stuff that this other servant had said.

He's left us on this planet and is testing us with the chance to get promoted. It's there for all of us, and we're going to make a decision. Do you know you were the one that was given the five talents? Do you know you are the one with the two talents? Do you know at least you were the one given one?

This is here for you. Don't look at God the way that third servant looked at God. Don't think, "I wasn't given enough," because the same process of promotion worked for all three, and it's according to our ability.

You're reading this book to gain in your ability. When you show Him that you have doubled what you've been given, then it says, "I will give you more," and He will let you keep what He gave you. This message is for you to say, "God, I agree with you. I'm going to make you proud." And as the other two servants came to Him and said, "Look what I've done," that's what I want you to do. "God, look what I've done. This is what You've given me, and I'm making the best out of it." Stop comparing your talents to other people. Stop looking at theirs to determine your value or the value that you don't think that you have. You must be grateful and say, "God, thank you. I'm going to cherish this, and I'm going to invest it, and I'm going to give it my best shot." Will you promise me you'll give that your best shot?

Do you know that God gave you at least two. Keep your eyes fixed on Him. Don't ever question why you're at where you're at. It's the same process of promotion, that if you are diligent and you work with the spirit of excellence, He sees what you're doing and the two were turned into what? Four! Then, if you keep going, the four turns into what? Eight. And the eight turns into what? Sixteen. Sixteen turns into thirty-two, and thirty-two becomes sixty-four. Have you gotten unfocused looking at other people's stuff, thinking, "They're better than I am. I'll never get to where they're at." No more. That is a lie from the pit of Hell. Don't you dare compare yourself to the one who has the five. You just keep going.

Don't compare. Take care of what He gave you. Trust Him with all your heart. Lean not on your own understanding, but in all your ways acknowledge Him, and He will direct your path. One day, you're going to look up and go, "Wow! I had no idea that I would ever get to this place."

Are you a five? There is a trap set for you and it's called the comfort zone. That trap is when you compare your results to other people, and you see yourself so far ahead of where other people are, that has been your gauge. Others cannot be your gauge because that gets you into a rut and into a comfort zone. Have you compared your results to other people and thought, "I don't have to work as hard because they're so far behind." Let me tell you something. That is exactly what the servant with one did. You have got to rise up with the five that He has entrusted you with and give it that spirit of excellence each and every day. Not looking to the right, not looking to the left, but keeping your eyes focused on Him, saying, "God, I'm going to get better this time. I'm going to go higher this time with you."

Don't fall into the trap of becoming the servant with the one, and burying your gift. No. He's given you a lot. It's time to make your Daddy proud. He trusted you with a lot. Now it's time to show Him that He made a good investment.

What number do you think I was? Do you think I was the one? I was not born with the five. I was born with one, and the one thing I had was a spirit of excellence. I gave it my best on a basketball court, and that's it. I was not born with gifts. I wasn't born with talents. I was born with the desire to give it my best. If this one, who spent most of my life underneath a rock, could rise up, then so can you. The same God that promoted me wants to promote you.

"I came home with more boldness, conviction, confidence and a better ability to communicate with my husband and children. When implementing the words 'obey', 'honor' and 'respect' in a loving posture with our children the response has been instantaneous!"

~ Linda K.

SIX TESTS TO DETERMINE IF YOU ARE READY FOR YOUR GIFTS

Goo says, "You are given gifts; creativity; administrative gifts; leadership gifts; just like I've been given those exact gifts. Neither one is better."

You may be called to be an apostle; you are a 'marketplace apostle.' No matter what you do, you won't get outside of that gift. You may be called to be an evangelist; you are a 'marketplace evangelist.' Are you really good in sales? That's an evangelistic gift. "Well, should I be out there saving souls?" Yes, while you're making sales. Lead by example. If you are in management, that's a pastoral anointing. Healings are happening in business seminars. Every single month, by the hundreds we see people dedicating their life to doing things the right way. People are standing up for what is right and living in that right place.

I hope to wake you up, shake you up, and help you open your eyes and realize that from the beginning of time you were raised up and trained up for such a time as this. It is not just for your glory it is for His glory. He gets the glory when you succeed therefore, you are called to succeed. It makes Him look good and He likes to look good. You dedicate what you have to Him, and

He will draw men right straight to what you're doing.

We find these tests by looking deeper into the story of Joseph. Let's look at Genesis 37. This is a story about business, promotion, tests in the promotion, after the promotion, and through the promotion. You are going to get a revelation; you're going to see the cheat sheet for the test.

Pay very close attention. Genesis chapter 37:2-11 says, "Joseph, a young man of seventeen, was tending the flocks with his brothers, the sons of Bilhah and the sons of Zilpah, his father's wives, and he brought their father a bad report about them. Now Israel loved Joseph more than any of his other sons, because he had been born to him in his old age; and he made a richly ornamented robe for him. When his brothers saw that their father loved him more than any of them, they hated him and could not speak a kind word to him. Joseph had a dream, and when he told it to his brothers, they hated him all the more. He said to them, 'Listen to this dream I had.

We were binding sheaves of grain out in the field when suddenly my sheaf rose and stood up right, while your sheaves gathered around mine and bowed down to it.' His brothers said to him, 'Do you intend to reign over us? Will you actually rule us?' And they hated him all the more because of his dream and what he had said. Then he had another dream, and he told it to his brothers.

'Listen,' he said, 'I had another dream, and this time the sun and moon and eleven stars were bowing down to me.' When he told his father, as well as his brothers, his father rebuked him and said, 'What is this dream you had? Will your mother and I and your brothers actually come down and bow down to the ground before you?' His brothers were jealous of him, but his father kept the matter in mind."

Genesis 37:12 says, "Now his brothers had gone to graze

their father's flocks near Shechem. So he said to him [Joseph], 'Go and see if all the flocks are well and the brothers with the flocks, and bring word back to me.' Then he sent him off to the Valley of Hebron."

Test Number One

Joseph is the second youngest of a large tribe, and he's favored by his father and gets this nice beautiful coat. His brothers hate him because they know that they are not going to be the heir of the father's tribe, of all its wealth, and all of his estate. So they're really ticked off at this kid. And the father protects him more.

Have you been in a situation where you've had somebody treated better than you? Joseph knows his brothers hate him and what does he do? He "casts pearls before swine," as some of us do on a weekly basis. You're telling some people the vision that God has given you, and the plans and purposes that you know He planted in you; and you're casting it before swine.

So, the brothers could not stand him, and, yet, here's a big giant character flaw. Now, check this out; it's really sad to me. Joseph had favor from his father and favor from God. The brothers also had favor; they were all princes of the same tribe. However, the other brothers are looking at what they don't have, instead of looking at what they do have. They're looking at the one thing that the younger one got, which was this ornamented coat. The other brothers are princes; they're wealthy; they have an inheritance. Yet, they're not satisfied with that because they are riddled with absolute envy. So what takes place, following this, is that Joseph presents his dream, the brothers hate him all the more. Why in the world would Joseph present this dream to his brothers?

He knows they hate him. Pride; what else? Ego; he wants to gain acceptance, and he wants to prove his position. He wants to gain acceptance from his brothers, and he's trying to prove that he has a position; that he's equal to them, if not better to them. That is total immaturity, and many of us do it every single day. We do it with our spouses; we do it with our bosses; in our churches; we do it with co-workers; we do it with people all over the place.

People trying to prove their authority; trying to prove who they are, and all they're doing is provoking envy and jealousy straight out of their brothers and sisters—which is exactly what Joseph did. He provoked envy straight out of those people, and all of his pride and ego, out of insecurity, trying to prove that he was something that he wished, he believed, he was to become.

What we find here is that he goes and he finds his brothers grazing the flocks. They see him from afar, and one of his brothers says, "Here come's that dreamer! Come now, let's kill him." (Genesis 37:19:20) They plot to kill their younger brother. So, instead, Reuben, who is the oldest brother, steps in and says in verse 22, "Don't shed any blood." Instead in an effort to rescue Joseph, Ruben suggests that they throw him into a cistern. Judah, one of his other brothers, then suggests to the other brothers that they sell him to the Ishmaelites and they all agree. Sure enough, they do; they throw him in a pit. They sell him to the Ishmaelites for twenty shekels of silver. They take the ornamented robe tear it up, and mangle it. They then sacrifice a goat and dip the robe in the blood of that goat. They wind up taking the robe to the father.

Now, here he is, favored son, ornamented coat, chosen to be the next heir of that particular kingdom. Doing what? He's a slave. Ego and pride; proving that you are accepted; trying to hide the insecurity, provoking envy and jealousy, leads to what? It leads to destruction of a dream. So he has these visions and, within days, he is in a pit; he is now bound-up as a slave, and off to Egypt.

The brothers bring the coat back to the father; the father covers himself with ashes; covers himself in dirt. He is just distraught, and he pretty much dies inside. He's just living out his days, but he is dead inside. His favorite son is gone. Before we move on in this story, I have to ask you something. Can you see how envy and jealousy leads to a malicious plot? Can you see how it leads to murder?

It led to murder with Cain and Abel. It leads to destruction; it leads to more lying, cheating and stealing, is what it does. I don't want to go any further until you clean "house." If you are battling with envy and jealousy; you are envious when you see other people succeed; envious when you see other people favored, you've got a jealousy streak in you. If this describes you, I want you to repeat this prayer after me.

"Heavenly Father, please forgive me for being envious of other people's favor; other people's success. I don't want to be that way; I don't like being that way. So, right now, in the name of Jesus, envy, pride, jealousy, get out. In the mighty name of Jesus, I am done with you. You have no power and authority over me; in Jesus' name, Amen."

When envy tries to rise up or cling to you say, "Shut up, and go back to Hell where you belong. That is not me; I am not an envious person. I am a new creation."

Envy and jealousy will only lead to the destruction of your vision, your dreams, and your goals. Envy says, "I have to take that person out so I can have what they have;" that's what envy does. It wants to destroy somebody else so that you can have what they have. If you get what they have, it will not last because of what was sown. Whatever you sow in envy, you will reap in envy.

Do you want to reap envy? Have you? Genesis 39:2-6. This

is so incredible to me. Here we have Joseph a slave. He is serving somebody else at this point, and the word says, "Now, Joseph had been taken down to Egypt. Potiphar, an Egyptian who was one of Pharaoh's officials, the captain of the guard bought him from the Ishmaelites, who had taken him there."

Look at what it says next. "The Lord was with Joseph, and prospered him." And it says, "And he lived in the house of his Egyptian master. When his master saw that the Lord was with him, and that the Lord gave him success…" Who gave him success? "That the Lord gave him success." Where does your success come from? From the Lord. If you are not serving Him, how are you going to get success? "You might be thinking, People succeed without the Lord all the time."

You're right because the principles work, but it says that "Whatever the laborers build without Him, they build in vain." Do you want to live in vain? Then you better live with Him. So, the text says, "When the master saw that the Lord was with him and that the Lord gave him success in everything." What does everything mean? "Everything" means everything.

I am reading from the Old Testament, which means that this was written in Hebrew, and guess what "everything" means in Hebrew? Everything. When your master sees that God is with you, and has given you success, then you will find favor in the eyes of your Master. The eyes of your company president, the eyes of your boss, the eyes of whomever.

So let's read it again. "When his master saw that the Lord was with him and that the Lord gave him success in everything he did, Joseph found favor in his eyes and became his attendant. Potiphar put him in charge of his household and entrusted his care—everything he owned was put in Joseph's hands." He went from a slave, prospered and was promoted to the head of the governor's household.

"Then one day, Potiphar's wife came"—and Joseph was a nice looking man at this point, and she was taken with him, so she makes a plot to seduce him. She makes a play when they are alone in the house. She says, "Come to bed with me."

He says, "Sorry. Your husband has entrusted everything into my care except for you, and I will honor my God and not touch you," and he leaves. So then she traps him again. She makes sure that there's nobody else in the house; it's just her and him. She says again, "Come to bed with me," and he says, "No." So she screams, "Ahh"; she grabs his cloak, rips it off of him, and he runs naked through the palace.

She screams again, "Somebody help me, somebody help me. This Hebrew is making sport of us. This Hebrew tried to seduce me, but I told him that I'm Potiphar's wife, and there's no way that I could do that." So she lies. Evil, wicked, liar, cheating, and stealing woman.

So Potiphar's wife comes, tries to tempt him, but he stands up under temptation. Tough temptation man. Do you think it would have been hard to stand up underneath that?

You're a slave, you have this vision and now, you're the furthest from the vision. You have this vision of being in charge of your whole family; being wealthy; having all this stuff going on. Now, you're a slave in somebody else's house, and some good looking rich woman comes after you saying, "Come on let's go to bed." He stands up under temptation, and he says, "Not going to do it; no way."

You see, he was going to be served in his dream. He was going to have people bowing down to him in his vision. In order for him to be promoted to that place, God needed to train him on a few things first. The first test was that he went from being a slave to serving in a foreign land, to a foreign man who does not even serve the same God.

He humbled himself and he served. Now, what is the proof? It says that, "God gave him success." You might interpret that he's sitting there in his recliner and then, boom it just fell on him. That is not how it works. If you read the Bible from cover-to-cover, there is a formula for success. Joseph did not sit there and say, "Oh, well, you know, who are these people anyway? These are just a bunch of heathens. They don't even serve the Most High God. They're just a bunch of Egyptians, you know, talking to Pharaoh, god on Earth." "They are not worthy of the work of my hands. Don't you know who I am? Don't you know I am Joseph?"

No, he learned how to serve somebody else that did not even share the same spiritual beliefs. When he was a young man, what did he do? "Serve me. I'm the best, I'm favored, and I'm the chosen son." He didn't have to go out to the flock. Daddy wanted him right by his side. Well, God said, "We're going to have to change some of that." So he winds up serving. My question to you is, "Will you serve no matter where you're at?" Joseph winds up going from Potiphar's house straight to prison, and, now he is in prison. Guess what happened while he was in prison? The Bible says again, "God gave him success in prison." The prison warden put Joseph in charge of everything. Now, he's gone from favored to slave to prisoner.

He was a prisoner serving criminals, serving people, who serve false gods. Do you think that would stink? So that's the first test; he learned to serve in becoming a slave from the protected son to prisoner. What will your attitude be when your vision seems so far away? Do you have a little bit of an idea that God has called you to freedom in every area of your life?

I will tell you something. Here he has the vision, and then, he's the furthest way from it. Why did God give him success? He had the attitude of the person that was going to lead. He did not stop serving his God. He did not stop honoring his God. He did not stop working with the Spirit of Excellence. He did not say, "Well, forget it then, it's not going to work. Why even try?"

He did not walk in laziness. No, he prospered where he was planted. You may have a vision. You may be thinking "I want to be successful. I want to build something dynamic." You have to act now, as though you are that already.

So whatever was put into his hands, Joseph worked as though he was leading a people. Whatever success God has given you right now, you need to treat that as though it is what you want already. That is what Joseph did. He has a vision, it's far away and he's a slave. He still sows into his gifts right now as though he was already the leader of a nation. Do you need to work on that?

Sadly, that's where most people fail. They think that once they get there it's over. It is never a "once you get there." It is the preparation "for there." Joseph was being trained, as a slave, to lead a nation. He was being trained; as a slave, as a criminal, as a servant, to, eventually, lead the most powerful nation at that time.

Test Number Two

Test number two is, he stepped up. He gave it his absolute best shot at whatever he was doing and wherever he was. The Bible says that we are co-laborers with Christ; you put your 50, he puts His 50. We're co-laborers with Christ. He who sows sparingly reaps sparingly.

So he gave it his best shot. There was no whining, complaining, murmuring, self-pity, pride, ego or "poor me." There was no blame. There was no shame. He knew who sent him, and he said,

"Okay, I guess I'm going to serve in a prison."

Have you been in situations where you wind-up whining and crying—even blaming God? Are you in a situation right now that you don't like? You may be blaming God for that situation, or blaming other people.

Here's what you need to realize: He has you exactly where he wants you, and where He has you, is where He wants to be teaching you something. So test Number One, again, learn how to serve even in the humble beginnings. Number Two, you have to step up and give it your best shot as though you were there already.

In the midst of a test; in the midst of a disaster; in the midst of things not going your way, what you are to do is to see it, to believe it, to walk towards it, as though it is already, as Joseph did. Prosper where you're planted. Treat the business that you have is though it is the successful business that you want. Treat your marriage/family as though it is what you want it to be. So that is a test. Will you give it your best shot in the midst of where your vision seems the furthest away?

Do you need to work on that? I'm going to tell you a quick story. I had lived in this house for five years; it was a condo – it was 2,000 square feet. When I bought it, it was my dream. I was 21 when I bought it. I went from homeless to a year later, living in this beautiful quarter of a million dollars condo. After a few years, I got tired of the condo and I wanted to move out, but the market had slipped so bad that if I sold it, I would have lost a lot of money on it.

So I had to wait for the value to come up. I used to complain and murmur about the house all the time. I didn't keep it up. I didn't decorate it. I didn't do anything with it because "I don't like this thing. I'm tired of this thing," and the Lord spoke to my heart through that story. He spoke to me loud and clear, and said, "If you treat this like the big dream house that you want, then the dream house will come."

How in the world can you be trusted with the bigger, nicer, house when you don't take care of the one that you're in? You're thinking, "Oh, once I get that house man, I'd have it spit shined. My toaster will be sparkling; there will be no crumbs anywhere." Have you thought this way? Do you have this mentality of "when I get there?"

No, you have to treat it as though it is already. Do you not like your car, and, therefore, you do not clean it? It's dusty, it's trashed, there's stuff broken; you just don't care about it. He is seeing how you are treating what He has already given you to determine whether or not you are getting promoted to the next level.

It is impossible to get promoted if you don't take care of what you've already got. That goes for the house; that goes for the husband. Many wives, many husbands, say, "I wish my wife was like this," or, "I wish my husband was like that." I used to do that with my husband, Hans. "I thought, I wasn't supposed to be married to some broke young kid that doesn't talk to anyone—there's no way. "How did I wind-up with him? I was supposed to be married to a multi-millionaire that didn't need my money."

This is what God said to me, "Really? How would you treat that person?" "I'd pamper him. We would have fun all the time. I'd have some awesome meals ready for him when he got home from work. I would look good all the time." And God said, "No, you wouldn't. You'd treat him the way you're treating Hans, right now, because you don't know how." This is what the Lord showed me. He gave me a vision of my husband standing before thousands, powerfully talking and teaching and training. He showed me this vision of my husband being everything that I wanted to be married to, and

God said, "As soon as you can treat him as though he is that multi-millionaire, then he will become it. Quit treating him like the 'warehouse man'"; which is what he was doing at the time. So, treat that husband or wife of yours as though they are already what you want them to be.

You speak life into the situation. As Joseph had a vision all around him he was saying', "I don't care. I am going to take what I have, and I'm going to practice right here." He was practicing on the slaves; he was practicing on the other criminals that were in that place.

The next thing that happens in the story is that there's a cupbearer and a baker that come; they get accused of stealing something from Pharaoh, the king. And Joseph interpreted dreams; he had a gift of dream interpretation.

He's in the prison cell, these two people come in, and they say, "We heard you interpret dreams." The cupbearer and the baker, also, had dreams, and, so, Joseph interprets these dreams; and, basically, the baker was the one that was guilty and was going to have his head cut off, and the cupbearer was the one that was innocent and would be restored back into his position.

Pharaoh is being tormented, night and day, about these dreams that he's been having, and none of the psychics can discern it; none of the seers can determine it; none of the magicians can discern it. No one has the ability to interpret this dream that he's getting because it was God Almighty Himself who sent the vision to Pharaoh.

So Joseph interpreted these dreams just like that. He said, "You're going to die in three days; you're going to be restored in three days." That's basically how it went. Well, sure enough, in three days, the proof came out. The baker's head was cut off and the cupbearer was restored. Joseph said to the cupbearer, "Please, remember me."

So, sure enough, guess what happened? The cupbearer forgot. Two years later, Pharaoh was having these nasty dreams, and the cupbearer forgot. The Bible says, loud and clear, "And God reminded the cupbearer."

When you're out there working, are you thinking, "Gosh, you know, no one is watching what I'm doing. Why am I going the extra mile because no one's paying attention to it anyway? You know, I never get any recognition for what I'm doing." You are trying to serve the wrong people.

You're looking for recognition and promotion from the wrong department; the wrong name on the outside of the door. You're looking in the wrong places if that's what you're doing. Joseph said, "Please, remember me," and the cupbearer forgot. So there he is, he's in the presence of Pharaoh, watching Pharaoh ask all these people and no one can interpret any of these dreams, and God reminds him.

The cupbearer goes to Pharaoh, and he says, "Your humble servant, please, I just have to let you know. I know somebody that knows how to interpret dreams." "So bring me this man," is what Pharaoh says. Joseph goes to serve this Pharaoh; he interprets the dreams exactly, and, basically, the dream was a financial message that there will be seven years of plenty in preparation for seven years of famine.

Seven years of plenty for seven years of famine. Are you in a season of famine right now? Or, are you in a season of plenty. If you are in plenty it is in preparation for famine. When you are in a famine you are preparing for plenty.

Are you stoked that you're in a famine right now? It's all about what you do in the famine that determines what the plenty is going to look like. Also, how you are in plenty also determines the discomfort of your famine. Do you know that Egypt became the most powerful nation of its time during the famine? Do you know that they made money during the famine? The favor that God put on Joseph made that nation prosperous. So while everyone else is starving, they're coming from afar to buy grain, trade grain, do whatever they can to get grain.

Famine hits, and there is Joseph's family off in a far land. They hear that somebody in Egypt has food. The father sends them with gifts and money, "Please go get some food." So they go to get some food, and guess who they have to get the grain from? Joseph. They don't recognize Joseph because he looks like an Egyptian.

He is tattooed; he's wearing a wig, he's wearing a dress, he's got gold necklaces on. Excuse me? You mean, God took one of his chosen people and put him in the heathen marketplace and had him look just like one of them. He had him speak their language; participate with their customs.

You mean, God tattooed the boy; God pierced his ears, and he was wearing a white dress with a gold flap? Look at how we look at the youth today, tattooed up, holes in their ears. We say, "That's not Godly, they need Jesus." Maybe, they have Him, and, maybe, they've been strategically placed, to lead other lost souls right to the Kingdom of Heaven.

God did it then, He's doing it now. Get your head out of your religious box. How in the world are you going to help them if you're acting like something they don't want to be?

So God promotes Joseph, a Hebrew. He interprets the dream of Pharaoh and Pharaoh says, "You are now in charge." He says, "You be the one that figures out how to solve the seven years of famine and the seven years of plenty." So he goes from favored son to slave in a pit; working in the governor's house; falsely accused to criminal serving other criminals that are actually guilty to second highest in command of an entire nation.

Pharaoh put him in charge of everything. Pharaoh, also, put him in charge of his household, and his entire nation. He entrusted, into Joseph's hands, everything. The Bible says every single time that he got promoted, it says, "And God gave him success, and God prospered him." Where does your success come from? Don't think for a minute that it comes from you.

We are co-laborers with Him; whatever you put out, He doubles it. You get good at putting out, He will, then, triple it. You get even better putting out? He will quadruple it. You get even better putting out? You're looking at a hundredfold. That's what it says. Do you want to be promoted? Do you feel like you are in slavery right now? Then prosper where you're planted.

Take care of the peanuts you've got and you'll get more. Do you feel like you're in prison, with a warden over you? Do you feel like you're in a dungeon? In that part of your life, what are you supposed to do? Prosper where you're planted; treat it like a beautiful garden, and you'll get promoted out of it. How do you go from criminal to head of an entire nation?

If you can be trusted with the small things, and you treat it as though what you will become, then guess what? God is the one that promotes you. He's the one that exalts the humble.

Test Number Three

Test number three, will you use your gifts in the midst of disaster? Will you use your gifts? Will you use them when you're discouraged?

Would you say that Joseph had every right in the world to be discouraged? Yes he did, but he didn't sit there and cry the blues. He wasn't lying on his back crying because all of his misery. He wasn't. What was he doing? "Okay, this is what I've been given; well, this is what I'll prosper with."

So will you use your gifts even in a bad situation? Will you use your gifts even when the vision seems like it's extremely far away?

Test Number Four

The fourth test is that he went to work right away. What if Joseph had not interpreted the dreams of the cupbearer and the baker? Opportunity always presents itself; the question is "Can you see it?" Well, you know what the definition of "luck" is? "Being in the right place at the right time and knowing it."

There are many people that will read this same book that you're reading, that will see it, that will catch it, will move forward and go after it. Will you be one of those people? Success is not on trial. Somebody's going to take action; that somebody can be you. Will you go to work when the opportunity arises to use what you have?

Are you going to read this book and do what happened when the cupbearer and the baker came to Joseph and gave him the opportunity to utilize his gifts? He was in a miserable situation, and the way that he kept his mind going was to he kept connecting with God, by seeking God and utilizing his gifts.

During discouragement, do you say, "Oh, phooey with it. I'm going to quit; it doesn't work anyway"? Have you done this? No more, you need to obey. Whenever you're going through a time of discouragement, or disappointment, guess what? You are facing a promotion. When you are going through discouragement and disadvantage and disappointment, you are being tested for a promotion.

That's what this story is showing, and only two percent of the population's is going—"Oh, great. Life is terrible; I'm going for it."

The other 98 percent of the population's going to whine.

"I had a vision and my brothers hated me, and they threw me in a pit. I was sold into slavery and then I was falsely accused. I'm still a virgin. I'm living in a prison. I just want to go home." Do you know someone like that—real close? I know it's not you. Are you in a disaster right now? Beep; this is a test.

Will you come through with flying colors? Do you know how loving our God is? He will let you take the test again. If you fail the test you're in right now, you'll have to take it again and again and again. Are you sick and tired of repeating the same test over and over and over again? He will chase you for the rest of your life.

You might as well stop messing around, get serious, get busy, get some skill, and get success already because that's the destiny of what's going to happen. Joseph did not blame; he didn't criticize; he didn't condemn; he didn't do any of that; he just said, "All right, I'm just here—I have to succeed no matter where I go. No matter how bad it looks out there, I'm going to give it my best in here."

Test Number Five

Here's test number five. So, now Joseph is successful: Egyptian wife, two children. The famine is here and their barns are full of grain. People from all over the place are coming to them. Everything's looking great, and all of a sudden his brothers show up to get grain.

He recognizes them, but they do not recognize him. He then reveals himself to them in humility. I have to take you to this place; this is just absolutely profound. In Genesis chapter 45 verses 3 through 11 it says, "Joseph said to his brothers, 'I am Joseph.'" Can you imagine?

You have sold your brother into slavery, and there you are

begging for grain. This man that looks like an Egyptian is standing before you. He takes his wig off, he speaks in his native tongue, and he says, "'I am Joseph. Is my father still living?' And his brothers were not able to answer because they were terrified at his presence." The guilt they lived with all those years.

"Then Joseph said to his brothers, 'Come close to me.' When they had done so, he said, 'I am your brother Joseph, the one you sold into Egypt'"—get this, "And, now, don't you be distressed, and do not be angry with yourselves for selling me here because it was to save lives that God sent me ahead of you. For two years, now, there has been famine in the land, and for the next five years, there will be no plowing and reaping, but God has sent me ahead of you to preserve you a remnant on the earth to save your lives by a great deliverance."

"It was not you who sent me here, but God. He made me father to Pharaoh, lord of his entire household and ruler of all Egypt. Now, hurry back to my father and say to him, this is what your son, Joseph, said: 'God has made me lord of all Egypt. Come down to me. Don't delay.'"

"You shall live in the region of Goshen, and be near me, you, your children, your grandchildren, your flocks and your herds, and all that you have. I will provide for you there because five years of famine are still to come; otherwise, you and your household will, be destroyed and destitute." He knew who sent him. There is no blame to the circumstances.

There is no blame, vengeance, anger, bitterness, resentment or unforgiveness—none. God used the brothers to train up this young one to not just be ruler over his own tribe, but over the greatest nation in the world at that time. The vision you have, that you can see, is much smaller that what the reality of what it will be.

The Bible says that, "No eye has seen, no ear has heard, no mind can conceive what God has in store for those who love Him." (I Corinthians 2:9) Do you know Him? Do you love Him? If you are being tested right now, you have a choice that is to pass or to fail. Will you know during those times of trials, that He was the one that sent you?

Is it possible to prosper during a famine? Yes—that's if you're wise during the "harvest time." If you're wise in the "plenty," you will prosper in the "famine." Are you tired of starving in the famine? So my question to you is when the time arises, will you forgive those that do not deserve it? Did his brothers deserve it?

Test Number Six

Test number six is amazing. This is a level of leadership that goes beyond most people I've ever seen in my life. In fact, maybe one or two examples ever, in my whole life of all the people I've worked with and studied, Joseph did not take any credit for his success. He said, "It was not you that sent me, but it was God that sent me." When he met with Pharaoh, Pharaoh said, "I heard you interpret dreams." He says, "I can't do anything, but God has used my mouth to interpret dreams."

At every opportunity that he used his gifts, he professed his frailness and said, "I can't do anything without Him, but He has given me a gift, and I will use it." When you get to that place where He has promoted you, there is another test. Will you give Him the glory or are you in it for yourself?

In test number six, will you give He who has equipped you; He who has put you in the right places; He who opened the doors; He who gave you favor; He who has made things happen for you; will you give Him the credit? Here's another thing, will you see the opportunities that are sitting right there in front of you? Most people do not.

Whether that opportunity is in the grocery store, in the bank, on your job, in your own house or in your ministry; if you do not use what you have been given, you will not prosper. Do you want to prosper? Then you must prosper where you are planted. If you don't like where you're planted you might curse where you're planted. "I'm so tired of this job." "I hate this job." "I'm so sick of this administration." "I can't stand this, and I can stand that."

You will never be promoted out of the situation that you are in by cursing it. You will only reap curses upon you.

In Thessalonians it talks about the criteria for an elder, and it says that for this person to be in leadership, you need to watch his family; and if his children and his wife honors him, and he can run his household, then, certainly, he can lead other people.

If he cannot lead his own family, then he certainly cannot lead anybody else. So if Joseph could not lead the prison, how could he lead a nation? If Joseph couldn't lead a household, how in the world can he lead a nation? Do you know what's so awesome about God? Look at the little bit that Joseph had to do.

He was trusted with peanuts and God brought the big time harvest. That's huge; so you must use what you got, with all you got, with excellence. You need to pass the test of trying to gain acceptance from your fellow man. You need to pass the test of trying to make people envious of you—trying to prove that you are worthy of their acceptance. Do you care about your acceptance? You want His and His alone.

He's already accepted you. It doesn't matter what they say or think. You have to pass the test of temptation of trying to prove that you're worthy; trying to prove that you've got something. Get over trying to prove it; you've already got it. You have to pass the test, vision to prison. "How will I act in that prison?" "How will I take care of my car?" "How will I take care of my house?" "How will I take care of my spouse?" "How will I take care of my kitchen?" "How will I take care of my business?" "How will I take care of my customers?" If you can be trusted with the small things, God multiplies it greatly. What an awesome God that He would give us the "rule book" in advance. Have you failed some of these tests?

Have you failed all six of them? I have. Here's the good news; you get to take them again. With your finances it's the same way. How you take care of your finances, where you spend your money, determines whether or not he can trust you with any more.

How in the world can He trust you with a $1,000,000 if you can't even take care of $30,000? How you take care of the $50 will determine whether or not it grows to $100 and then $500 and then $1,000,000. This is not rocket science, but what an awesome God that He's given us that chance to know those tests.

Ask God now to forgive you for the places you have failed. Forgive yourself while you are at it as well. And then, get ready for your next promotion in life.

"This has changed EVERYTHING! I can no longer continue on the path I was on. Thanks to you, I realize that my crossroads is TODAY! I am lining myself up with destiny. Thank you for opening my eyes!"

~ Sarah T.

BECOMING ONE OF GOD'S CHOSEN

Y GOD HOLDS as a promise to us, and He says if you do this you can test Him on it. I have tested it and it is true. It has to do with wealth and abundance.

I don't know where you are right now in your life. I don't know where you are with God, but if you plan trying to do it without Him, you're going to have some hardcore challenges. I'm not saying you're not going to have any challenges with Him, because you will, but it's so much easier when you have the big "G", God on your side.

Do you often feel overwhelmed with what you feel inside you and what you want to do? God has a word for you concerning that. In the book of Matthew it says, "Many are called, but few are chosen."

Are you a little bit confused about that scripture? I was when I first read it. I would hear that scripture and to be quite honest with you, I felt that I certainly was not chosen and I wasn't even qualified to be called. Those were two groups that I was not worthy of, and why? Because I felt like, according to the church system, I would never, ever measure up to be used by God.

Have you felt the same way? My husband and I would sit in church and they would announce all of these things: hey, come volunteer for this, come volunteer for that, and if you're really chosen by God, then you will be a youth minister or a Sunday morning preacher.

If you're really called by God then you would start some kind of a ministry, whether it's feeding the homeless or scrubbing toilets as a janitor. That this is what it meant to be a Christian? A part of the reason I didn't want to be a Christian was because I thought God would put me in a brown robe and send me to Russia to sing. My gift is speaking, not singing. No, thank you. I didn't want to do something like that, and that's one reason I stayed away from God for five years. I then came to this place of total emptiness, and after I exhausted the whole metaphysical world, I came to a place of yearning and emptiness, and I re-dedicated my life and something got filled in.

Many are called, but few are chosen. Let me break it down and make it real plain to you. Imagine basketball tryouts. That's the many that are called. There's a calling, an invitation for basketball tryouts, but few are chosen.

Two boys show up. One boy is the hotshot from last year and says, "I've got this sucker in the bag. I don't even have to work hard. Look at my competition, shoot, I got it." Boy number two is eager. He's got his new shoes on, shorts, t-shirt; he's ready to play his heart out. He is double dribbling, he is granny shootin' it. He's fouling people, he can't get down the court dribbling the ball right, but he's hard working, willing, teachable, and he's hungry. I have a test for you. Who gets chosen? Let's find out.

In 1 Samuel 16:6, Samuel was told to go to the house of Jesse to anoint one of Jesse's sons as king. He walks into the house, sees this big, burly, beautiful man and says, "That guy looks kingly, he must be the one. He's the eldest son, he's strong and he's good looking. But the Lord said to Samuel, "Do not consider his appearance or his height, for I have rejected him." The Lord does not look at the things that man does. Man looks at the outward appearance. God looks at the heart.

So, who gets chosen? David did in the Bible, but who gets chosen on the basketball team? The pig-headed, unteachable kid who thinks he's got it in the bag? The one who doesn't need any help and says, "Don't tell me what to do." Or is it the kid with no skill, but a great heart? Yes, the kid with the great heart gets chosen. Many are called, but few are chosen. Who gets chosen? The hungry, the teachable and those who have desire. The ones who are willing to do what it takes to make it.

Many are called, but few are chosen. The 12 disciples, now that's quite a group of people. If I were Jesus, would I choose them? Think about it. If you were Christ and you're looking for people to start your mission with, would you choose them? Of the 11 who denied, who doubted, who did not believe, who were unfaithful and ran at the cross. He spent three years with them and they took off. Is that who you would pick? It's obvious that God chooses differently than man does. When it came to the disciples, God knew their heart. We see this throughout the entire Bible. The way it works is that many are called. There are tryouts, right? What happens after tryouts? A team gets chosen. What happens with that team after the team's been chosen? Preparation. Preparation for what? To win, of course.

Prepare to Win

Are you called to lead? What determines whether or not you're chosen to lead? Your heart. What determines whether or not you will lead? The preparation. Let me show you how to prepare to lead.

You see preparation with King David. David was prepared as a warrior. He was a warrior in the marketplace. He was not a priest. Caleb was not a priest. Isaac was not a priest. These were not preachers or pastors, they were kings in the marketplace.

The Bible says some are kings and some are priests. King David should be your model. He was a warrior, he was a worshipper and he was a king. It seemed to be a pretty good formula.

David knew how to get things done. He was totally abandoned, fully surrendered to the Most High God, and he inquired of the Lord on everything.

David was the apple of God's eye even though he was an adulterer. Even though he was a murderer, he was the apple of God's eye. God promised that He would establish His kingdom in David forever. His kingdom is still on this earth today; I am part of that kingdom. And if you are a follower of Christ, you are also part of that kingdom. That kingdom has stood for thousands and thousands of years.

Many are called, few are chosen. The preparation for David to be a warrior began when he was a shepherd boy with the bear and the lion. The preparation for David to be king involved serving and submitting to another king. He served and he submitted to somebody else's vision before his vision came to pass. He was anointed king at 16 years old. Do you get overwhelmed with the idea of destiny? That's because you think you are supposed to make it happen.

In your current state you can't make it happen. You are in the shepherd boy stage. Of course, that destiny seems huge and mighty. God told David, "I will establish My kingdom in you forever." That would be a little intimidating for a 16 year old kid right? David was thinking, "Look at my brother, he looks like a king."

Let's look at the preparation of Jonah. I know this one personally, and once in a while I wind up back in the belly of a stupid whale. God tells Jonah to go to Nineveh and give a message. Jonah rebels, "I'm out of here, I'm going to Tarshish." The Lord had something for Jonah to do. Jonah ran from what he was supposed to do because he thought it was something different than what it really was. You might be running from what you are called to do. Let me tell you. He will chase you down for the rest of your life.

We see preparation throughout the scriptures. Esther was prepared. Every one of them was prepared through opposition, conflicts and trials. Are you going through some conflicts? Trials? Earthquakes? Tribulations, as they call them? Through these they were prepared for what was to come.

Do you believe that you are called to lead? There are several different areas that you have got to be prepared in if you plan to lead people. Let me help you with a few.

1) Learn How to Deal With People.

If you don't deal with people properly, they are not going to want to follow you. They are not going to want to listen to you. They are not going to want to obey and submit. They are not going to want to be directed by you. If you don't know how to deal with people, there's nothing you can say that will make them follow you. In fact, the people skills that you have right now may make people run from you.

Many are called to lead, but few will step up, learn and be equipped on how to deal with people. Very few will make that investment. Very few will submit to God in that way.

Dealing with people, obviously pulling out the best in them is an art. It is not easy. Have you heard the scripture that says love one another? Do you really know what that means? Do you really know what it means to love one another? I'm not talking about surface love. I'm not talking about loving the easy ones. I'm talking about loving the ones that drive you crazy!

I know there is scripture that says to love one another, but that is something that is a challenge for me. I must lean on Philippians 4:13, which says, "I can do all things through Christ who strengthens me." I need to lean on this scripture daily to love other people. If you don't know what it means to love one another, remember this scripture. You need Christ to love people.

Why? Because people can be mean, manipulative and rude. They gossip and they judge. Do you see how easy it can be for people to hate other people? Without God it's a lost cause, trust me. Love is actually a fruit of God. It can't happen without Him.

2 John 1:6 says, "And this is love, that we walk in obedience to His commands." I'm sure you have heard that His command is to walk in love. What is love? 1 Corinthians 13:1-7, says, "If I speak in tongues of men and of angels, but have not love, I am only a resounding gong and a clanging symbol. If I have the gift of prophecy and can fathom all mysteries and all knowledge, and if I have faith that can move mountains, but have not love; I am nothing."

If I can become a millionaire and lead a large group of people, and I don't love, I have nothing. If I give all my possessions to the poor and surrender my body to the flames, but have not love, I gain nothing. Love is patient. Just think about that for one second. Love is kind. It does not envy. It does not boast. It is not proud. It is not rude and it does not say, "Oh, this is my favorite." Love is not self-seeking. If you are self seeking you will scare people away. As I said, you need to learn to love people because it does not come natural to any of us.

Love is not easily angered. It keeps no records of wrong doings. Love does not delight in evil, but rejoices in truth. Love always protects, always trusts, always hopes and always perseveres.

Galatians chapter 5, Verse 13 says, "You, my brothers, were called to be free." "But do not use your freedom to indulge in simple nature. Rather serve one another in love."

2) Conflicts and Trials

If you plan on leading a people, then you must learn how to deal with conflicts and trials. You need to understand their purpose. Most people freak out and fret. Hebrews says, "God disciplines us for our good that we may share in His holiness. No discipline seems pleasant at the time. Discipline however produces a harvest of righteousness and peace for those who have been trained by it."

James 1:2-6 talks about considering it pure joy when you suffer painful trials. It says the testing of your faith develops perseverance. Perseverance must finish its work so that you may be complete, lacking in nothing.

Be honest. Do you usually freak out when it comes to trials? Do you usually fret, blame someone else or blame yourself for the trials? Or maybe you curse the devil for it. Sometimes it is the devil and sometimes it is God disciplining you. How do you know? It depends on if you are dealing with the consequences of your own choices or not.

What I am referring to is dealing with the consequences of your own crap. If it is not the Devil, then it must be Daddy. In the past, I have been disciplined in two different ways, by my health and my pocketbook. That's how the Lord spanked me. I had a heart attack at age 24, a nervous breakdown at age 25 and a fatal heart condition at age 30. You might ask, "God did that to you?" No, I pretty much did it to myself. It was just the consequences.

Have you ever spanked your children? The scripture says, "Spare the rod, spoil the child." Do I really believe that? Absolutely, I have five children and I will tell you spanking works, no question. I don't beat them like I was beaten, but will definitely give a swat where and when it is needed. This is done in love of course, explaining, bringing them to correction with a heart full of repentance. I have a system that I follow. They recognize it when they see that look in my eyes. They know, its time to obey. It's a healthy, reverent fear. It's not the kind of fear I had of my dad. That was a hateful fear. As a mom I don't want them to have that kind of fear.

That's your Daddy in Heaven. In Hebrews it tells us "Don't be upset about it. When He spanks you it means that He loves you." He only disciplines those He loves. Consider yourself a son or a daughter of God if He's disciplining you.

Are you one that can't get away with anything? Me neither. It is actually part of my name, the name that has been prophesied over me my entire life means God is my judge. "God is my judge," that's what Daniel means. That means a short leash. Do you have a short leash? For example, you cannot speed without getting a ticket? That is a major short leash. You cannot lie. You can't fib. You can't tell a white lie. That's a short leash.

3) Who Are You Following?

To whom are you submitting? To who are you held accountable? If you cannot submit to man, you will not submit to God. The Bible says for us to submit one to another, it's that simple. If you're the maverick out there doing your own thing by yourself, you have no one holding you accountable. You don't have anyone you can trust. You're trying to make it out there on your own and you're in trouble. You're heading for a fall. I'm not suggesting that you have just anyone hold you accountable as that can be a disaster. You need someone that you know has your best interest in mind.

How you follow will determine how others will follow you. If you are the type that says, "I don't need to follow anybody," it should not surprise you that you have a bunch of people around you that won't follow anybody either. How you follow or how you don't follow will determine how others will or won't follow you.

4) Bridle Your Tongue

Finally, in preparation for leadership you need to bridle your tongue. By reading this book you are being equipped with a very powerful level of leadership. The most crucial part is becoming an effective leader.

Proverbs 18:21 says, "Life and death is in the power of the tongue and you shall eat the fruit of it." You see, if you speak death over people by making statements such as, "they're a bunch of lazy, unteachable, unwilling people that don't follow directions," you speak death over your crop. You just put poison on your crop. Life and death is in the power of the tongue and you shall eat the fruit of it.

You might say, "I just have ten lazy people." If that's how you treat the ten, do you think God's going to trust you with the 20, or 10,000? If you speak death over 100, do you actually think that's going to earn you the right with 1,000? No!

How you treat what you have right now will determine whether or not you pass go and collect $200 or if you go straight to jail and have to try again, and again, and again, and again, and again. Where are you?

5) Choose to Believe

You have to choose belief over doubt. You have to choose action over procrastination. You cannot try to overcome it. You have to step in and say, "I'm going to do this." What happens when you set your mind to it and your mouth follows? Your feet begin to move in the direction they're supposed to go. There is no, "I just can't seem to motivate myself." Get up and move. If you just open your mouth and begin to speak it and then you follow your speech, success comes. You don't need to read a book on procrastination. You don't need to read some book on fear and opposition and how to overcome it. Just start speaking life. Start agreeing with life. Start agreeing with action because your feet follow your mouth.

6) Submit to God

What does that mean? When I first heard submit, I heard it in the form of "submit to your husband." Submit doesn't mean what you think it means. The word "submit" means to respect and honor.

There is something that Hans and I had even during our time of hating each other. We had a deep, passionate love for one another. We still do to this day. You can ask our friends or anyone on our staff. We passionately love each other. Sometimes that passion turns into an argument, but it always ends in some fun. That's the important thing.

So, when I learned that submit meant to respect and honor, I wept and said, "Wow, I love him passionately. I hate being around him. I hate the way he does things. I hate this and that." At the same time I had this deep, passionate love. Have you ever been in that situation? When I learned that submit meant to respect and honor, I realized "I do not respect one ounce of this man and nor do I honor any part of who he is."

I treated my clients better than I treated my husband. I respected my clients and I respected perfect strangers more than I respected my husband.

Wives submit to your husbands, it took an act of God for me to do that, a huge miracle.

So submit to God. Job 22:21-22 says, "Submit to God and be at peace with Him. In this way prosperity will come to you." Accept instructions from His mouth and lay up His words in your heart.

Do you feel a calling to lead? If you do not pray you are stupid. Who do you think brings the people? He does. If you are not inquiring of Him, do you think He can trust your influence over them?

I don't want to take a chance. We are so blessed that God has placed over 100,000 clients in our hands. Wouldn't you say that's a pretty big level of influence? I had to be trusted first. I failed a few times in the beginning, but then I figured some things out. First, I can do nothing apart from Him, as I have submitted to Him, prayerfully seeking Him, prayerfully inquiring of Him. What do I do next? Where do You want me to go? How do You want this done? Give me a sign, show me confirmation. I'm not doing anything without You. I don't want to be anywhere where You are not.

That's my prayer every time I step up to do a seminar. "God, if you're not there, I'm not showing up on that platform."

Do you live like that? I haven't always lived like that. I used to depend on myself and my talent and my ability to succeed in life. I don't anymore because it leads to destruction. If you're not tapping into the source of your talent, you will run out. Then, there you are, left high and dry, like I was. Not being able to function, not being able to talk. Not wanting to use any part of my gifts.

God is the one that plants the desire and He's the one that also takes it away. You may be thinking, "How does this person who speaks life, encouragement and equips people get into a depression?" I was doing it in my own strength and talent, putting trust in my ability, putting trust in my personal experience to become a millionaire, and it ran dry. Have you ever run dry before? It's not fun, is it? No matter what you try and no matter what you do, you can't seem to pull it together.

That's when you know you're leaning on your own strength and not the strength of the Most High God. If you are leading a people or you feel called to lead people, and you are not submitting to God and praying daily, you are being stupid.

If you want to get to where you want to go, then you need to start submitting and bowing down to your God, daily. Apart from Him, you and I can do nothing. There are a lot of hurting people, and there's a revival taking place in the marketplace. There is a renewal of God's spirit penetrating walls, boundaries, borders, people, and races. He needs an army, He's developing an army who will go out and fight the good fight of faith, who will go out and represent and glorify His name. That doesn't mean you go out and get your license to be a minister. I have one and it's just a piece of paper on my wall.

You have the same authority that I have in Christ. It is the same authority and the same power. You have access to all the same Bible, the same principles. It's up to you. Will you not submit to Him? Will you not fully surrender all and not care about the outcome? Can you do that? Time will tell.

Have you ever been in a situation where somebody has forced you to submit? Would you say it's not fun? God doesn't make you submit, He gives you the choice. When I chose to submit to Him, miracles began to occur in my life.

7) Ask for Help and Pray for Miracles

Pray for miracles over your people. You have a people just as Moses had a people. You have a people just like David had a people. You have a people as Abraham and Isaac and Jacob. Israel had a people. That's what you have. You might have five, but you have a people.

You need to start seeking God whole-heartedly and fully surrender, not conditionally, not half hearted, not with a halfway commitment, not only when you need Him, but fully abandoned. Do what it takes to be chosen. When the choosing comes around, you are the one with the right heart. You are the one with the right work ethic. You are ready to be chosen.

"Prior to Dani's training I was bound up spiritually, emotionally and financially. I was raised with a poverty mindset that caused me to subconsciously sabotage every effort I made to become successful. Dani has given me a completely new mindset about success. I have been set free in every area as she has spoken truth over my life. I am living in complete freedom and victory with the ability to run, without hindrance, towards the future I know God has for me. I now am bearing fruit as a Christian while I am living in the fullness of all that God has created me to be."

~ Stephanie B.

GIVE GENEROUSLY

D O YOU HEAR a calling to be financially blessed? Proverbs 15:27 says, "A greedy man brings trouble to his family." Would you like to know what breaks poverty? Giving breaks poverty. I am not going to give you all this information about giving and then guilt you into sending me money. I don't need your cash. I am not a broke pastor. I am not a broke missionary. I am a wealthy one and I didn't make my money from taking offerings. Please don't read this as pride. My boast is in my God who is faithful to His word and His principles. I have never taken an offering. I have been sent to give to the needy, not take from them.

Do you know about the concept of giving? I am sure you have the same measure of faith that I do, and you rob God weekly, monthly, and yearly, and you're expecting to be insanely successful in your career, your family, in your ministry. Not going to happen.

The wealthy know the concept and live by it. Its God's Law just like the law of gravity. Let me help you. In 2 Corinthians 9:6 it says, "Whoever sows sparingly will also reap sparingly, and whoever sows generously will also reap generously." A greedy man brings trouble on his house. He will have poverty at the end.

Would you hate to make a ton of money and lose it all? That

would be lame wouldn't it? Mathew 13:4-9, explains reaping and sowing, and the different types of soil. Do you remember the four types of soil we talked about? Clay, rocky, thorny, and the last one is fertile.

Only one soil is fertile. There is only one soil with a promise and the promise is 30, 60, and 100 fold return. That is fertile ground. If you've been sowing in rocky, thorny or hard clay ground, that's why your investment has not reproduced itself. The only way to get the 30, 60, and 100 fold blessing on what you have sown is to sow it into fertile ground.

How do you know if what you are sowing is fertile ground? Whether or not souls are being saved. That's how you know. Where is the money going? Where there is fruit being produced? You might attend a dead church and have not grown in 25 years. Dead. You're sowing into that ground, and things are not growing back to you. Why? It's clay and nothing grows in clay. Nothing grows in sand.

How do you know if it's good soil? There's good fruit. There's good fruit. If you call yourself a good Christian and you are sowing when they pass the plate and that particular organization is not working under the great commission which is "go ye all to the earth preaching the Gospel," winning souls, casting out demons, healing the sick, blind eyes seeing, deaf ears hearing, lepers being cleansed and captives being set free.

How do you know what is good soil? By the fruit. Reading this book, you obviously sowed into fertile ground based on the fruit. What is the fruit? The results! God has brought us thousands of results from our clients.

The reality is that most people don't sow anything anywhere. That's the truth. Do you know that only 2% of the church actually tithes? Isn't that sad? That's why they're broke.

Luke 6:38 says, "Give and it will be given to you. A good amount will be poured into your lap." You need to underline this in your Bible and post it on your ceiling. "Give and it will be given to you. A good amount will be poured into your lap. It will be pressed down, shaken together, and running over. The same amount that you give will be measured out to you."

Since we have been giving into the Kingdom of Heaven; the poor and needy, the widows, the children, and the gospel used to preach with souls being won into the Kingdom, I have gone through seasons of less than, but never ever had a need for anything. In my retirement, I walked away from a three quarter of a million dollar a year income. Do you think that had an impact on me and my family? Huge, but guess what happened during that time? It was pressed down, shaken together. When something gets pressed down, doesn't it have an appearance of it being smaller? When your trash bucket is full, don't you press it down so it has an appearance of there being less? Why? So you can put in more.

You may be going through that right now. You may be in the pressed down stage at the moment, and that's only if you're giving. If you're not giving you're being disciplined financially. If you are not sowing, you are being disciplined for not sowing. If your finances aren't growing, it's because you're not giving. That's one reason. Another reason is you aren't working. If you aren't working, the income isn't going to grow. It's that simple. Remember, that's chasing a fantasy.

Another one of my favorite scriptures is Malachi 3:10. Malachi 3:10 has this promise that says, "Bring the whole tithe," 10 percent of your income, "into the storehouse, that there may be food in my house. 'Test me in this says the Lord." He's saying that if you bring Him ten percent, you can test Him. He says, "and see if I will not throw open the floodgates of Heaven and pour out so much blessing that you will not have enough room for it." It's not about a church. It's about where there is good soil, it is reproducing itself. It is true storehouses produce fruit not deadbeats in the pews taking up space leaving the same as they came in.

He who helps the poor will be blessed. He who turns his face against them will have many curses upon their heads. Is your organization helping the poor? I will tell you that tithing has to be in the name of Jesus, and wherever that tithe goes it has to be done in the name of Jesus. Yes, it could be anywhere. You should prepare to succeed because you're always going to get what you are prepared to receive.

The Bible talks about giving generously to the poor and the needy. Be careful not to harbor wicked thoughts. Don't give with a grudging heart because the Lord, your God, will bless all your work in everything you put your hand to do. God loves a cheerful giver. If you obey willingly, then you get a blessing. If you are being manipulated to give then the giving is futile. Give in obedience to Him, not manipulation of man!

It says in everything you put your hand to do. What does everything mean in the Greek? Everything.

What if you don't put your hand to do it? Then it certainly can't be blessed. There's a blessing already waiting. If you don't put your hand to it, you will not receive it.

Here's the truth and I'm going to stand on this truth. You own nothing. God does not need your money. It has nothing to do with you giving money. It has everything to do with the condition of your heart. In the last chapter we said that "Many are called, but few are chosen." If you give generously and obey the Word of God, the Lord says test Me on this. I will press it down, shake it together, and make it running over. Test me on this, if you sow it into good soil, you will reap a good harvest. Test Me on this, I will bless everything you put your hand to if you take care of the poor.

It's already in motion. He owns it all anyway. It's a heart condition. A stingy man will have his share of poverty. If you are stingy and you don't give, and if you call yourself a child of God and you are not giving ten percent, you're heaping curses on your head. Trust me. I learned this the hard way. I used to think it was all mine and when it came time to pass the plate I was not happy with putting thousands of dollars in the bucket. I didn't like it. It wasn't until my heart changed that I got fully, ridiculously, pathetically, obscenely blessed, and it continued to grow.

I am floored at how much we have the privilege of giving away in the name of Jesus, not DaniJohnson.com, every single month. It brings me to my knees every time.

You don't own anything. Your kids are on loan. Your car is on loan. Your house is on loan. Your body is on loan. Your spouse is on loan. Your friends are on loan. It's nothing but testing ground and preparation to see what you do with what you have and to determine whether or not you are ready for the next step.

If your ten year old child came to you and said, "Daddy or Mommy, I have a dream, I want to drive a race car 150 miles per hour." Are you going to hand them the keys? No! They are not prepared. Your Father in Heaven will do the same things with you.

Your Father is not going to put you in your destiny unless you are prepared for it. If you are having a hard time with it, then that's between you and your God.

"It's one thing to create an income, it's another to live out your destiny and what you are supposed to do in the world and how we can impact it."

~ Bryan A.

REFINER'S FIRE

I WANT TO GIVE you a secret, a shortcut that I found in scriptures. In fact, a humongous shortcut that has made me a tremendous amount of money, saved me money and saved me from making giant mistakes. It has helped to open doors for us that no man can close and shut doors we're not supposed to go through. It has been a secret for protection, a secret for prosperity, a secret for debt reduction and a secret for absolutely everything. Would you like to know that kind of a secret?

When I was 18 I walked away from God and the church. I said, "God, if I have to be like your people in the church, then I want nothing to do with you. I had every reason to feel like I couldn't trust people that were in organized religion. However, eventually I realized that I was judging those people and had to ask forgiveness for the thoughts I had against them. I now love the church whole-heartedly and have a passion to help people overcome any hurt or rejection they may have experienced. I want to see people succeed instead of being led in different directions.

Do you struggle with being afraid of what your future holds? Do you worry about it? Do you wonder about it? You're just not sure where you're going?

If you're uncertain about your future, I want you to have your eyes opened about where you're supposed to go, what you're supposed to do, etc. I believe you have an innate desire to succeed in business and in life, because you have a 'Kingly' anointing.

I have a question for you. Do you think God wants you to have success? I believe that God wants to build His Kingdom and I believe that He's going to use the kings and the priests to do it. But if you don't know who you are or what your rights are in the marketplace, how will you take it by storm?

Purify Your Life

I want to talk to you about a process of refinement that you are going through whether you know it or not. It says in 2 Timothy 2:20, "In a large house, there are articles not only of gold and silver but also of wood and clay. Some are for noble use and some for ignoble use. If a man cleanses himself from the latter, he will be an instrument for the noble purposes, made holy, useful to the master and prepared to do any good work."

Would you like to be used for a noble purpose? Whether you are silver, gold, wood or clay, do you want to be used for a noble purpose? Would you like to be a part of a big, good work? Do you want to be a part of something awesome that makes a difference? Most of us do. You're about to and you don't realize it.

So what is 2 Timothy saying? If we cleanse ourselves, then we will be put to use by the master for a good purpose. Timothy talked about silver and gold. Some of us are silver and some gold. In order for gold to be made precious, the same applies to silver, it has to be refined. The word refined means, "To make fine or pure, free from impurities." Did you catch that? Would you like to be free from impurities? Free from 'dross'. Do you know what dross is? When silver is being heated up, it is the dross that actually rises to the top. It is scum formed on the surface of molten metal, waste matter, worthless stuff, rubbish. That's what the dictionary says. It says, "Purify, clarify, to free from imperfection, coarseness, crudeness; to make more subtle or precious."

In other words, the jewelry that you wear on your body has been refined. If it has not been refined, it turns green, in some cases dark gray, if you're wearing silver. That means it hasn't been refined. All the impurities have not been brought out of it. So, being refined is basically a process that brings forth purity, the best. It gets rid of the junk so that the best, the priceless, the precious stuff can come forward. Most people are afraid of the refining process. They're absolutely afraid to look at themselves. They're afraid to look at what needs to be changed. They'd rather ignore it, and they go through life in absolute bondage, never reaching the full freedom and fullness of what they're called to be.

In 2 Timothy, when it talks about noble use, in order for it to be used nobly, the refinement process has to happen. In order for you to get what you want, the refinement has to happen. So what am I saying? Have you been through hell? Have you been through some hard times? That is the refinement process.

Have you failed over and over again? Have you been tested financially several times by the Lord? This is not an accident. Have you made a lot of money and lost it? This is not an accident. You're going to be refined so that the next time you make money, you keep it. We gain resources during a recession, that's how it works. However, that's only if you have been refined through this last process.

I'm going to talk about clay for a little bit. Isaiah 45:9 says, "Woe to him who quarrels with his maker." Does the clay say to the potter, "What are you making? Isaiah 64:8 says, "Yet, oh Lord, you are our Father. We are the clay. You are the potter. We are all the work of Your hand." Jeremiah 18:6 says, "Like clay in the hand of the potter, so are You in my hand." This is the Lord speaking to you. 2nd Corinthians 4:7 says, "But we have this treasure in jars of clay to show that this all-surpassing power is from God and not from us. We are hard pressed on every side but not crushed. Perplexed but not in despair. Persecuted but not abandoned. Struck down but not destroyed." Have you felt perplexed and confused before? Despair comes from the pit of hell but if you're in the will of God, you are not in despair. How awesome is that?

Talking about clay, wood, gold and silver, and the refinement process, we're going to get uncomfortable. We're going to get very uncomfortable. I want you to imagine that you are a lump of clay and you're in the Master's hand. So here you are, and here He is with His wheel and He has this lump of clay. Now He is trying to form who you are to be. Have you been poked a few times? Prodded and stretched? Would you say that the refining process is uncomfortable? Yes, it's very uncomfortable. Do you have any idea what a pot has to go through in order to become a beautiful piece of art? It goes through the fire. So, the Master sits there and pokes you and presses you and stretches you, and slices you and dices you and rips you into two. During this process are you whining and crying, and complaining and screaming?

Have you ever kneaded bread before? Can you imagine being that poor little lump of dough? You might have gone through this before. If you haven't, guess what? You are about to. Now let me tell you why.

Refinement

When that thing is formed the way the master wants it to

look, then this jar or this pot now goes into the fire. Why does it go into the fire? For refinement. What happens in the fire? It brings up the bad stuff. So why aren't there more people submitting themselves to the fire of God? Is the bad stuff really that great? We live in a lie that says, "I don't want to talk about that. I don't want to deal with that stuff. No, I'd rather live in this lie. It's more comfortable over here."

So God refines the bad stuff, puts us through the fire that purifies the bad stuff, then we sit on the shelf. Have you ever been benched by God? Are you hitting your head up against the wall in your life no matter which way you turn? You've been benched. The stuff that needs refining has to sit on a shelf for a certain number of days then, guess what happens? They take it off the shelf and its back in the fire again.

Is this your life? You're poked, you're prodded, you're ripped in two. You're sliced, you're diced, then you look beautiful, and you're like, "I got it. I made it. I have arrived." Have you ever been there before? Does it hurt? Is it hot? Is it uncomfortable? Then He sits you down and says, "Shut up and wait, because I'm not done with you yet." Brings you back up, heats you up, hotter the second time, and then you're ready to be used.

Are you willing to get the junk out? Are you willing to say, "All right. Send me through the fire. I am done with my dross. I'm done with scum. I'm done with the bad. I'm done with the junk. I can't go on in the way that I'm going on." Are you ready for that?

Five Areas of Refinement

There are five areas that have to be refined in you, in order for you to: succeed wildly in the marketplace, carry the favor of God, get the next raise instead of somebody else that doesn't deserve it, be exalted, whatever it is you desire. You have to humble yourself before Him.

1) **Unfaithfulness**—Proverbs 13:15 says, "The way of the unfaithful is hard." Do you like hard ways? Me neither. Proverbs 11:6 says, "The unfaithful are trapped by evil desires." You might be thinking that the word unfaithful means an adulterer. Yes, it does talk about it in that way, but unfaithfulness is a little different.

Do you have a conditional commitment to your success? Conditional means, "If everything goes right, then I will work it out. If I have some people that say yes, then I'll keep going. As long as the company doesn't make any changes, I'll stay." That is conditional living.

Faithfulness is faithfulness, is faithfulness, is faithfulness. Who are you serving? Why are you here? What are you doing? I don't know about you, but I'm here to serve the one that created me. That's who I'm here for! I'm here to do whatever He wants me to do. If He wants to just put me in a brown robe and have me sing in Russian, which no one wants to hear me sing, then I'll do it. I'm willing to do whatever. If He wants me to be poor or if He wants me to be wealthy, sign me up. I don't care. All I know is wherever He is, that's where I'll be satisfied.

Conditional commitment, conditional love for your children, conditional love for your spouse. That's not what this is about. It is about unconditional attitude.

Are you unconditional to people around you? If you're going to be used mightily where you are at, you cannot be unfaithful. You have to be faithful. If you are faithful to God, He is faithful to you. If you're not tithing, if you're not giving ten percent straight off the top, you are not being faithful to He who gave you what you have. That is one area.

If you're going to be in the marketplace and you're going to carry the banner of Him, and you are going to have the favor of God, and He's going to make a way where there is no way, He's going to open doors that man cannot open, then you better be faithful to Him. You better be faithful to your spouse. You better be faithful to your kids. You better be faithful to serve Him first and Him alone. Not to serve money, not to serve greed. There's only one that deserves the highest position, and that is Him. Not me, not anybody. So faithfulness is one area.

2) **Ungratefulness**—This is so huge. The definition of the word ungrateful is: not thankful for favors. When you look up the word ungrateful in a thesaurus it gives you the synonyms: offensive, atrocious, disgusting, evil, foul, hideous, horrible, horrid, loathsome, nasty, nauseating, obscene, repellant, repugnant, repulsive, revolting, sickening, unwholesome and vile.

Ungratefulness is what took the children of Israel and kept them in the wilderness for 40 years. It was the spirit of ungratefulness. Ungratefulness leads to murmuring and complaining. Remember, when the children of Israel murmured and complained to Almighty God, they provoked His anger. He wanted to kill them all. He hates that.

I want you to look at your life right now. If there is any place in your heart where you are ungrateful, say, "God, help me. Show me. Where am I ungrateful? Where do I have higher expectations on people than I need to? Where do I have higher expectations on myself or on my business that I'm not supposed to have?" Do you have it in your mind that it's supposed to be like this and when it isn't, you are a little pill to live with? Always looking at the bad, always looking at what's wrong, always looking at what's not working fast enough.

It is impossible for you to be blessed by God when you ungratefully receive a blessing from Him. How likely is He to give you another blessing? How likely is He to give you more favor?

3) Coveting—Romans 13:9 says it best. "Coveting implies a greed for something that another person has that they rightfully possess." A lot of people, and this is where it stands, covet other people's success. They covet other people's bodies, their figures, the way their body looks. They covet other people's recognition. They covet people's homes, people's spouses.

The grass is always greener on the other side, but it's just as hard to mow. It's the truth. If you can't keep your lawn mowed, what makes you think you could keep that lawn mowed? Coveting is a huge problem in the marketplace and a huge problem for Christians. It looks something like this: "I want to be where they're at." "I want their car. I want their house. How come they're the ones always getting all the recognition? How can I get that recognition? I want to be looked upon just like them." Do you know why Lucifer fell from Heaven? He wanted to be just like God. So his whole plan of attack on every one of us is to get us to want to be like somebody else, and that eventually leads to the very same place that he lays right now, in the pit of Hell.

Coveting is a state of never being satisfied with what you get, never being satisfied with results that you work so hard for. I had this all over my life. The first million that I had made, guess what? It was nothing to me. It was like, "Big deal." It wasn't as good as I thought it was going to be. So guess what the next goal was? "Gotta make another million. Gotta go better, faster, harder."

4) Idolatry—Colossians 3:5 says, "Put to death therefore whatever belongs to your earthly nature: sexual immorality, impurity, lust, evil desires and greed which is idolatry." It says here in the Word that idolatry is greed. Greed is idolatry. Idolatry, from the Greek, says, "Idol and to worship or serve. The worship of idols, images or anything made by hands or which is not God. Excessive attachment or veneration. Veneration, the highest degree of respect; reverence, respect mingled with some degree of awe; a feeling of sentiment, excitement by the dignity and superiority of a person by the sacredness of his character. For anything that which borders on adoration."

Idolatry is the worship of idols, excessive devotion to or reverence for some person or thing. I had to get deliverance from idolatry because it was prevalent in my life and I didn't even know it. Man is exalted in our culture today. Professional sports and athletes, celebrities and Hollywood. We have teens with pictures of half-naked women in their room that they worship because they are thin or beautiful or rich or popular. They literally bow down to them. In my bedroom, growing up, I had a full, floor-to-ceiling picture of Larry Bird. I had an entire wall, it was all Larry Bird. I had everything Boston Celtics. I idolized those basketball players.

Idolatry is huge in America and becoming that way around the world. We idolize movie stars. We idolize speakers. We idolize pastors. We idolize our spouses. We idolize anybody that looks like they are better than us. We hold them up in the highest of esteem.

5) Greed—The Bible clearly says that idolatry leads to greed. Why? Because greed has a way of lassoing itself around our necks and moving us faster and harder, "I've gotta have more. I've gotta have more. I've gotta get better." "More, more, more! Faster, faster, faster!" Ever deal with that? That was me.

If you're going to be led mightily in the marketplace, and you're going to absolutely wage war out there and take some serious plunder, you better be worshipping the right big "G" God and not the little-g god. The little-g god is called greed. The little-g god is man.

If you are obsessing over things—money, fame, your career, any of that stuff, it is a road to absolute destruction. I know I've been down the road myself. I lost everything twice because of idolatry and greed. It had me lassoed around the neck and I didn't know it. That is why I've been sent to warn you.

You're being prepared. You've gotta deal with this stuff. I had to because it is my heart's desire to change and impact the lives of millions of people all over the world, to stand up for what is right, to go after their visions, to encourage them to be all that God has called them to be. However, if I'm easily led by money, can you see how that would lead me down a path that wouldn't be to helping people? It would be to a path of absolute destruction.

Those are five basic areas in which you need purification, if you want to succeed wildly in the marketplace. If you want to succeed, then you absolutely have to be freed from all of those areas. The Bible says in Ephesians 5:5-6 "For of this you can be sure: No immoral, impure or greedy person- such a man is an idolater- has any inheritance in the Kingdom of Christ and of God. Let no one deceive you with empty words for because of such things, God's wrath comes on those who are disobedient. Therefore, do not be partners with them." Why? God is jealous for your good. He wants you to succeed. He wants you to be blessed and blown away by what He is going to do for you. He loves you so much more than you can imagine. Since He is a loving God, He wants you prepared so that you will do and be the best you can be and achieve what your heart desires.

He did it for me—He will do it for you!

"Spirit Driven Success has impacted me in so many different ways. In the way I think about my business, my marriage. I was lost on my path and trying to make God my personal friend and Savior. This series has clearly shown me a way to do that. Thank you so much!

~ Tammy

THE WEAPONS OF OUR WARFARE

FEAR IS A weapon used by the enemy against you with the dart of anxiety. Have you battled with worry now and again? That is the hand of the enemy shooting a fiery dart towards you. However, as the Bible says, our struggles are not against flesh and blood. They're against the principalities of darkness in the spirit realm. That means you do not fight worry with flesh and blood.

You fight worry with faith. Faith in you? No, faith in Him. He overcame the world. He died on a cross and rose again after three days. He overcame sin and death. He can overcome your mortgage payment. He can overcome your mouthy teenager. I don't care what you're facing. Heart problems are easy for Him. The question is are you using the weapon of your flesh and blood or are you using His weapons for war?

Faith is a weapon. Let me give you a couple more. Trust in God is a weapon used against the hand of the enemy. When you trust Him, you'll move out in faith. Obviously, David did not fight with his own strength. He fought with the strength of the Lord. Isaiah 41:10 says, "Do not fear for I am with you." This is the Lord speaking to you. So, "Do not fear, for I am with you. Do not be dismayed, for I am your God. I will strengthen you and help you. I will uphold you with My righteous right hand." That's what it says. If you're looking at your American Express bill, thinking, "This is so big" Even if its $50,000, He makes a way where there is no way. So, how long are you going to let worry, fear, and anxiety be a weapon that can be used against you? The choice is yours.

Matthew 9:18-30 reads "While He was saying this, a ruler came and knelt before Him." Here it's talking about somebody coming to Jesus. "My daughter has just died, but come and put your hand on her, and she will live." Jesus got up and went with him, and so did the disciples. Just then, a woman who had been subject to bleeding for 12 years came up behind Him and touched the edge of His clothes. She said to herself, "If only I could touch His cloak, I would be healed. Jesus turned and saw her. 'Take heart, daughter.' He said, 'Your faith has healed you.'"

Is faith not a total weapon against sickness, death and stinkin' disease? He rose people from the dead and said, "Your faith has healed you. Your faith has restored you." Continuing in Matthew 9, verse 22 says "And the woman was healed from that moment on. When Jesus entered the ruler's house and saw the flute players and the noisy crowd, He said, 'Go away. The girl is not dead, but asleep.' But they laughed at Him." She was dead, but He said, "Oh, no, no, no, no. She is not dead. She is but asleep."

Can you imagine laughing at the Messiah? Could you imagine crucifying Him? Verse 25 says "After the crowd has been put outside, He went in and took the girl by the hand and she got up. News of this spread all over the region. As Jesus went on from there, two blind men followed Him, calling out, "Have mercy on us, son of David! When He had gone indoors, the blind men came to Him and He asked them, "Do you believe that I am able to do this?" 'Yes,

Lord,' they replied. Then He touched their eyes, and said, 'According to your faith, it will be done to you,' and their sight was restored."

What about Abraham? In Romans, Chapter 8 and, Hebrews, Chapter 11, Abraham is talked about. He was 100 years old when he had his promised child, Isaac. It says that Abraham did not even consider his age and he did not consider the deadness of Sara's womb. Sara was 80! And they had been promised a child. A child that would give birth to another child, that would give birth to children, then eventually, his descendents would be innumerable. That was the promise that was given to Abraham.

Are you considering your current circumstances to determine your future? If you are, that's a plan of attack from the enemy from the pit of Hell. Because the truth is you have to walk by faith and not by sight. It says Abraham did not even consider. He did not look at Visa and MasterCard. Why? It will make you afraid, that's why. He did not look at I'm failing in my business. He did not do that. He did not even consider. Oh, I'm sure he saw it in his peripheral vision. He was 100 years old, still getting it on with his old wife, expecting a child. Yeah right, whatever.

"Come on, honey, we got a promised child to produce." They'd been doing it for a good 60, 70 years and she still never got pregnant. God still promised, and by faith he believed. Instead of, "Oh, what's the use. It ain't going to work anyway?

By the way, God thinks very highly of sex. He says, "The marriage bed is undefiled." Do you want to know what God thinks about sex? Read the Song of Solomon. I'm telling you, it's steamy. He likes you to have sex with your spouse, and only your spouse. He blesses it. You go!

So, are you considering your circumstances to determine your future? You go ahead and you keep your eyes fixed on Him.

"I have called you. I know the plans I have for you. I have a plan for you, and that is for good health, that is for success, that's for prospering. God is asking, "Will you agree with Me? Or will you agree with your adversary?" Who are you going to agree with?" That's what it's all about.

Don't you dare consider your circumstances to determine whether or not you're going to go for it. Don't you dare consider your circumstances to determine whether or not you're going to make it. Don't you dare consider your circumstances to determine whether or not you're worthy, whether or not you're good enough, whether or not you have enough talent. All of that stuff will burn. Just consider your God who is faithful, who has called you, not by accident, but by absolute purpose to go into the marketplace and wage war against what the enemy has stolen from you. You go and you take back what was promised to you because if you don't take it, they will. They will sow it into pornography, illicit sex, and children's pornography. They will sow it into more debt and more idols.

Not His people. Don't let your impossible circumstances determine what you do. The Israelite army consisted of adult men. In the story of David and Goliath, Goliath said, "I'm going to kill you guys. Come on, give me somebody." And what did it say? "Saul and his army were terrified." The king and his army were terrified. They considered the circumstances. Did David consider the circumstances? He says, "No way. You know what? You just insulted God. Ooh, you're going to pay for this."

Attack without hesitation, and fight with the strength and the weapons from the Most High God not the weapons of flesh and blood. Fight with spiritual forces of faith.

Walk by faith and not by sight. It also says that whatever you ask for and believe you will receive. Let me tell you something. In Matthew it says, "Ask and it will be given unto you. Seek and you shall find. Knock and the door will be opened unto you."

The Bible says faith without works is dead. Why? Faith is action. You cannot say, "I believe, I believe, I believe. Oh, I'm not going to make it. But I believe." It says ask by faith and believe and you will receive. Seek. Why? Seek is action. There are a whole lot of people asking in their prayer time from their God, "Please get us out of debt. Please Lord, get us out of debt. Oh, Lord, please get us out of debt." It says ask and have faith. Faith without action is dead.

Do You Know Him?

King David trusted God. He had faith. How did he trust God? How did he have faith? He could trust God because he knew Him. He knew God and so he could walk by faith and not by sight. Psalms 92:5 says, "How great are Your works, oh Lord, how profound Your thoughts." The senseless man does not know. Fools do not understand.

Do you know Him? Do you trust Him? Do you say, "God You brought me here. You gave me a desire to succeed. You designed me to succeed. Oh, Lord, I trust You. I believe I am destined for success." That is not to say that the road isn't going to be bumpy or that things aren't going to be hard. Oh, they will be, I promise you. It is to equip and train you to become better, to be given more. You see, the Word of God says that he who receives the Word and puts it to use, which measure they use it in will be given unto him. So, what measure you take from what I am giving you with this book, and the measure in which you use more will be given to you. Do you know Him?

John 15 is one of my favorite passages. It says, "I am the vine, you are the branches. If a man remains in Me, and I in him, he will bear much fruit. Apart from Me, you can do nothing. If anyone does not remain in Me, he is like a branch that is thrown away and withered. Such branches are picked up, thrown into the fire and burned. If you remain in Me and My words remain in you, ask whatever you wish, and it will be given to you." You might be afraid to ask. Why? You're afraid He won't give it to you. That's a lie from the pit of Hell.

Why would Satan want you to believe that God will not give it you? Well, if you believe then you would get it, that's why. Let me tell you about the weapon of Satan. It's called deception. Whatever he can do to get your attention off the Most High God, he will do. Whatever he can do to distract your mind to believe in fear and worry and anxiety, he will do. If you focus on those distractions you will not accomplish what you were set on this earth to accomplish. However, if you believe in what John 15 states, now you are a weapon used against the kingdom of darkness.

You may be afraid to ask. Not only was David not afraid to ask, he just didn't hesitate. Don't hesitate. Have faith. Trust in the Most High God. If you remain in Him, He will remain in you. And He, the strength of Christ that dwells within you is stronger than he that is in the world. He that's stronger than you is stronger than debt, sickness, death, and disease. Stronger than your mouthy teens, stronger than your boss, stronger than our government or politics.

So, my final question to you is, do you know Him? Do you know Him like David knew Him? Do you trust Him the way David trusted Him? Do you have faith like David had? Could you use some help in those areas? Do you know the Creator of the universe? Do you know the Creator of the Heavens and the Earth? Do you know the big "G" God, not the little g—god? Do you know the Wonderful Counselor, Almighty God, the One who is slow to anger, rich in mercy, and compassionate? Do you know the Gracious One? Do you know the Lord God Almighty? Do you know the One who parted the Red Sea? The Healer, the Provider, the Ever Present Help in time of need? The Redeemer? The Majestic One? The Holy One? The King, who laid His life down for you and me? Do you know The King of Kings and the Lord of Lords? Do you know the One Who Strengthens you in your time of need? Do you know your Shield, your Protector, your Comforter, and your Refuge? Do you know Him?

Life and Death in the Power of the Tongue

And finally, to prepare to lead you need to bridle your tongue. Proverbs 18:21 says life and death is in the power of the tongue and you shall eat the fruit of it. You see, if you speak death over people by making statements such as, "they're a bunch of lazy, unteachable, unwilling people that don't follow directions," you speak death over your crop. You just put a killer on your crop. Life and death is in the power of the tongue and you shall eat the fruit of it.

Prosper where you're planted. How you treat what you have right now will determine whether or not you pass go and collect $200 or if you go straight to jail and have to try again, and again, and again, and again, and again. Where are you, my friend?

James 3:5 talks about controlling a horse with a bit, a small little piece of metal. A ship is a huge vessel with a small rudder. James describes the tongue as an evil fire. He describes it as a world of evil among the parts of the body. It corrupts the whole person, sets the whole course of his life and itself on fire. The tongue is a restless evil full of deadly poison.

James also says, "It's a restless evil that no man can control." But what's the answer? The answer is that with God all things are possible. Apart from Him we can't bridle our tongue. With Him, our tongue submitted wholeheartedly to Him, it can be bridled. Have you tried to control your tongue on your own?

Do you have a challenge with speaking death over job, over your own life, over your business, and you can't figure out why you don't experience growth? I'm going to show you something very powerful. Matthew 12:36-37 says, "But I say unto you that man will give an account on the day of judgment for every idle work spoken. For by your words you will be acquitted or by your words you will be condemned."

This is serious. Do you know what the word idle means? It means careless. I looked up idle in the dictionary and idle means inactive. It means dead, unfruitful, barren, ineffective, and benefiting no one. We will be held accountable on the day of judgment for every ineffective, every barren word. What does barren mean? It doesn't produce fruit.

We are always speaking something. Isn't that true? Are you speaking life or are you speaking death? Are you speaking blessing or cursing—worthless, idle, careless words that benefit no one? Or are you speaking God's word that benefits all?

I speak God's word all day long, some in the form of correction and rebuke, some in truth of lifting people up and calling them to something much higher than where they are and what they are doing. In love and in mercy. This is something I have to work on myself. I have to literally bridle my tongue with the help of the Holy Spirit because I can't do it on my own.

Have you ever heard of Morris Cerullo? Morris Cerullo has traveled around the globe, and has affected millions of people on the planet. He's been a minister and a speaker for sixty years. He wrote a book called *The Battle of the Tongue*, and I highly recommend that you get a hold of it. It's a great read, lots of truth. One of the things Morris mentions in his book is that neurologists have proven that the speech center of the brain has total dominion over all the nerves in your body. It has absolute dominion over your life.

I want to tell you something. There is no commitment in trying to make it in your business. There is no commitment in trying to lead well. There is no commitment in trying to become wealthy. There is no commitment in trying. None. Either you will or you won't and that is determined by your mouth because your actions follow your mouth.

James 3:9-12 says, "With the tongue we praise our Lord and Father and with it we curse men. You have been made in God's likeness out of the same mouth come praise and cursing. My brothers, this should not be. Can both fresh water and salt water flow from the same spring? My brothers, can a fig tree bear olives or a grapevine bear figs? Neither can a salt spring produce fresh water."

God is very serious about your tongue. We were created in His image and through His mouth He spoke and we are here. He spoke and the Heavens and the Earth were created. He spoke and man was created. He spoke everything above and beneath the earth was created. We are created in His image, but we have not been equipped to use this tongue to create. We've used this tongue to destroy. It has to stop for much has been given, much is required, and now is the time to bridle this tongue.

Life and death are in the power of the tongue. Let me tell you the words and the way that the enemy speaks to you so you can learn what it sounds like.

He speaks through condemnation, confusion, through judgment, and criticism. He speaks through fear, guilt, and shame. Has he spoken to you personally? The enemy speaks through hopelessness. He speaks through resentment and blame. He speaks through torment. He speaks through intimidation. Can you remember the feeling of being intimidated by a person? That is from your adversary not to open your mouth confidently and speak life. Life and death are in the power of the tongue.

Have you been intimidated by your business, marriage, what to do with the kids, ministry? Anything that stops, thwarts, stands in your way, tears down—comes from where? It comes from Hell. He speaks through depression, and oppression. He also speaks through pride.

Let me tell you how pride works, which is why it's important for you to know the Bible. It's a nice little whisper that sounds like this: "You are so awesome. You are so good at what you do. Just look at you. You should get more recognition than what you get. You are the one that belongs on that stage. You are so good there is no one like you. There is no one in this entire company better than you. You're the best." That is pride. Putting yourself down is also pride. Whenever you are the focus, that is pride.

Your Father in Heaven speaks to you. It is in a similar way, but it is not those words because there is no one like Him. There is no one like Him and He is the only famous one, and He is the only one who can satisfy. And apart from Him, we can do nothing. That is the truth.

The enemy speaks through false humility. False humility says "I'm really not that good. No, I'm not that good at all. Oh, thank you, thank you. But, really, I gave it my best shot, but I'm really not that good." That is false humility. That is someone who has figured out that saying, "I know I'm awesome," is not good, and figured out how to say the same thing with different words.

Someone gives you a word of encouragement. They have spoken life over you. You are to receive it humbly. "Thank you so much for that encouraging word," and let it rest right there. Do not let the enemy run away with that encouraging word.

The enemy also says "Everything is always unfair. Nothing ever works out for you." He speaks through unfairness. He will show you that someone got promoted and you did not. He will tell you that it should have been your turn instead of their turn. Life is always unfair. The enemy speaks through unfairness.

He speaks through anxiety, stress, he speaks through doubt, and "You can't." He speaks through "You're not good enough." Here's a good one for you, he speaks through procrastination. He speaks through apathy and inactivity. He speaks through distractions. He speaks through passivity. He speaks through indifference. "I don't care. What's the use?"

He speaks through heaviness, self pity, and through retaliation. Lucifer and his little lies. He speaks in lust. He speaks in greed and he speaks in hate. Those are just to name a few.

Let me tell you about the voice of our King, the Most High God because you need to know His voice and the Bible says "my sheep know the voice of their shepherd." Your spirit knows His voice and your spirit desires to hear Him loud and clear. You've spent too much time turning your ears to your adversary and agreeing with what he has spoken with you instead of turning your ears to agreeing with your God.

You've been listening to the wrong side for so long. Let me turn on your ears. Your Father in Heaven speaks through grace. He speaks through mercy. He speaks through hope, and he speaks life. Your Father speaks through love and peace. Your Father speaks through faithfulness. He urges you to have self control. He speaks through joy, abundant joy. He speaks through patience. He speaks through goodness, kindness, gentleness. He speaks faith. He speaks encouragement. He speaks you can do it, I believe in you. Now go!

Now, the enemy likes to use the word "go" as well, but let me tell you what the enemy's go sounds like. Go, go, go! Go, go, go, go, go, go. Any of you ever hear that one before? That is the enemy. That is pressure and intimidation. That is torment. That is not the voice of your God. Go, go, go, come on dang it, go. That's not God.

The last thing that your Father in Heaven speaks through is a spirit of conviction. Let me tell you what conviction is. The devil cannot create anything, but he is the great counterfeit. Condemnation is the counterfeit of conviction. Condemnation puts you down. "You stupid idiot, you are lame and you better not get up again." That's condemnation.

But conviction says I made a mistake, I better make that right." Conviction makes you take a step forward to correct whatever needs to be corrected and you are built up in conviction. With condemnation you are torn down. So your Daddy speaks with conviction. Conviction, leads to freedom. Don't ever be afraid of going before the throne of mercy and grace and making a confession, saying, "God, search my heart. Know my ways. There's something in me that needs to change, let's deal with it now." Why? His convicting spirit raises up, it doesn't put down.

Have you submitted to condemnation far too many times? Send it back to the enemy the next time it wants to rise up.

The enemy speaks through intellectualism and reason.

"Noah, build me an ark." What the heck is an ark? They did not have a body of water. They didn't have any boats. Noah did not sit there and say let me do some research on that. He did not look up ark. He did not go to the library and pull out some encyclopedias on ark on the internet. He did not go study water. He did not say well, wait a minute, according to my calculations, it has not rained in, let's see, ever. According to my calculations there is no place to put an ark. By the way, how big is it supposed to be?

No, God said, "Noah, build me an ark" and Noah obeyed. The enemy wants you to reason obedience away, reason action away, and reason faith away.

So you need to direct your tongue with purpose. Psalms 17:3 says, and this is David who is my greatest hero in the Bible next to Jesus. "I am purposed so that my mouth will not transgress." Do you know that you have had a problem in the past with your tongue? I have watched tongues destroy entire companies, entire families, 20 year long relationships all because of the tongue.

There's nothing more destructive than a tongue. Such a small thing, but such a huge weapon. It's time to use that weapon for you instead of against you. It's time to use it against the enemy instead of for the enemy.

King David's kingdom is still on this planet and has been reigning now for 3,000 years and it will be a kingdom that reigns for eternity. Would you like to have a kingdom like that? Then purpose your life the way David did. He was a warrior, a worshipper, and a king who said, "I purpose my mouth that it will not transgress." One of the things he focused on was making sure his tongue agreed with his Father in Heaven instead of his tongue agreeing with his adversary. If you read through Psalms you'll see times where David is saying, "Help me God. I'm going to die."

When you're in the throne room, say anything you like. "God, I'm afraid, I don't know if I can make it, but I put my trust in You and You promised that I would be like a tree that sprouts all year long and that its leaves are always green. You promised. So I put my trust in You."

You need to work on your tongue. You need to speak what is edifying and strengthening. You need to speak what builds up, not what tears down. You need to speak on purpose. Even if it doesn't look right, even if it doesn't sound right, do it anyway. Life and death is in the power of your tongue.

Guard Your Mind

In the Bible, the word nike appears 17 times in the New Testament. Nike is a Greek word and means already victorious, not something you will be, not something that you might become, not something that is in the future, but nike means now. It is already victorious right now. I'm going to prove it to you.

The bottom line is "You are already victorious." Remember He planted a desire, it proves the design which then proves your destiny which is already there. Will you not have your tongue agree with this message? The only thing stopping you at this point is what comes out of your stinking mouth. I am going to help you. I am going to equip you to protect your freedom.

He said, "I died to set you free for the sake of being free." Do not return to a yoke of bondage. Resist the enemy and he will flee. Stand firm in the faith. That's what it says. I will help to teach you how to guard your home, which is your mind, and to stay free from captivity. I have four steps.

Four Steps to Guard Your Mind

Step 1

First, you need to pray, which is another powerful weapon. Seek Him first at all times. He delights in those who diligently seek Him. When you have truly sought Him out the delight that you feel is immeasurable. There's nothing to even compare it to, and I mean absolutely nothing.

James says that no man can bridle his tongue unless he submits it to the Holy Spirit. Let me teach you how to pray. I don't want to assume that you know how to pray. If I'm going to equip an army that's going to be deadly against the kingdom of darkness in the marketplace, then you better be a person of prayer.

Number one, I believe that you should start with praise, with worship, and thanksgiving. All of that is life, so that's number one.

In Psalms 34:1 David says, "I will extol the Lord at all times and His praise will always be on my lips." Praise, worship, thanksgiving is how you open with that time of prayer. I don't care if it's for 1 minute or 5 minutes, or 20 minutes. In fact I don't care if that's all you do through that entire time. You're breathing life over you. It's out of the overflow of the heart that the mouth speaks, and if you can praise and work in thanksgiving and worship to Almighty God, you will have nothing but life.

Now does that mean you won't have disaster fall all around you? Of course not, after all this is called planet stinking earth, but guess what? When you have praise on your lips you know that there is a Savior, a Redeemer, a Reconciler, a Faithful One. Your Comforter, your Strong Tower, that's what you know. So there is no worry, fret, and fear, it is "Lord I trust You."

Philippians 4:6 says, "Do not be anxious about anything." This is how you will keep your freedom. If you have a tendency to agree with anxiety, stress, frustration, and worry, memorize what I'm about to tell you. Do not be anxious. Is that a suggestion? No, it's a command. Do not be anxious about anything.

Here's the answer, by prayer and petition with thanksgiving present your requests to God. That is the answer for stress, worry, anxiety, frustration. Do not be anxious for anything, but in everything by prayer and petition with thanksgiving present your requests to God.

Step 2

The second area that you want to pray is confession. After I praise, and again this is just a guideline. Do whatever you want, there's only one thing you must do when you pray, and that's my final thing. But this is one thing that, I choose to do. If I want to lead, I want a clean heart, clean hands, I better do this, and that is confession. That's my time to confess before my God. Lord, search my heart. Is there something I need to be forgiven for, or is there someone that I need to forgive? Is there somebody that I need to bless with my mouth?

When there's that struggle in my heart over someone who's harmed or hurt or spoken something wicked against me, or have taken offense to something I have said; I have to lay that at the feet of my Jesus. If it takes root in me I am in bondage. Do you hate bondage? Me too. So destroy it with confession and forgiveness.

Step 3

The third thing you need to do is petition. Ask Him. Whatever it is, the Bible says all over the place "ask." I did a whole study on the word ask and it's in there so many ridiculous times it would take you forever to read it all. It's not 'ask' with an asterisk or a footnote. It's not ask "only if," no, it doesn't say anything like that, but it says ask. John 14:23 says, "I will do whatever you ask in My name so that the Son may bring glory to the Father. You may ask for anything in My name and I will do it."

What does anything mean? Anything. What does whatever mean in the Greek? Whatever. Whatever means whatever, and anything means anything.

So, number three is a promise. Jesus promised, this is Him speaking in John 14:14, "I promise I will do whatever you ask of Me so that my Father in Heaven will be glorified." It's a promise, not a suggestion, not a might, and it's not a should. It is a promise. So, you know how I pray? You promised, you promised, just like my kids. "You promised we were going to go to Disneyland. You promised that we would have ice cream after dinner. You promised we were going to have tacos for dinner tonight."

By the way, the Bible says to ask in the name of Jesus. You have no power or authority unless you use the name Jesus. If you are not praying in the name of Jesus, what you have spoken was a waste of your time, and a good chance that some other god, actually they're not all knowing and all powerful, but any demon that might have been around the block somewhere and caught word of what you asked for, you're letting the wrong side hear your petition. You must ask in Jesus' name, and it says to come boldly before the throne of mercy and grace knowing that you are a child of the Most High God and you have His ear. It says His arm is not too short, His ear is not deaf. He hears the cry of his people. That's what it says. So do you believe or not? Will you agree with your God who wants to bless you or not?

Step 4

Lastly, you need to now agree and believe. You have got to discipline your tongue just like an athlete disciplines their body and diet in order to win. They play to win. They do not get on the court all frumped out. They do not eat a cheeseburger and super size fries and milk shake and then get on the basketball court and play the game of their life. You can find this in Corinthians where

Paul actually talks about athletes conditioning their bodies to win. You must control and condition your tongue to speak life to win.

You need to weigh faith versus feelings or feelings versus fact. You see, we live in a world that caters to people's feelings and we set up bondage for them. Feelings are nothing more than a road sign as to what is in your heart and what has been planted. You have to size up the feelings to your faith, to the Word of God, to the truth. If it doesn't match up, I'm going to teach you what to do with it, and what you do is you say "go to Hell where you belong."

In spite of your feelings you have to choose to walk by faith and not by sight. It doesn't matter how you feel, life and death is in the power of the tongue.

Tell your feelings to shut up. If it doesn't line up with the truth that has been spoken over you, if it doesn't line up with the truth that is in the Bible, it is a lie and has to go to Hell. You have to choose to act on faith and not your feelings.

The Bible does not say he who walks by feelings and not by sight. It says to walk by faith.

You have to choose to speak life instead of death. Faith is something that is hoped for, the evidence of things not seen. The feeling may say in you, "I don't know, oh gosh, I may be success-ful."

Even when you don't feel like it's going to work, you walk by faith. Even when you don't feel like it's worth your time, you choose to do what you're supposed to do. It is about making a choice. When-ever you say, "I can't," or, "I couldn't," you have bowed down to bond-age. That's the truth. I can't or I couldn't. That is the language of a victim. That somebody or something else is in control of you.

Regardless of what your feelings are, you have to make a choice. I choose to make it. I choose to believe that His burden is light and His way is easy.

So, you have to agree, and you have to choose faith. You have to choose faith over excuses. You have to choose faith over problems, circumstances and reasons. It's a choice.

Next under faith versus feelings—do not give room or provision. Romans 13:14 says, "Do not give provision to the enemy." Interesting word; provision means to supply. Provision means to make due preparations. Provision means to arrange, cater, plan, to fix up with. Not only does it say resist, but it says do not give provision for, meaning the enemy is knocking at the door.

The Bible says to take every thought captive and make it obedient to Christ. You have to start thinking about what's in your head.

It says, "Take every thought, captive, and to make it obey Christ." So, this is what you do. When you finish reading this book you are going to have thoughts come at your head. Why? The enemy is going to try to test, he's going to try to come in, he's going to try to plant some little seeds of doubt, little seeds of fear, little seeds of rejection, little seeds of this, that, and the other thing. Your job is "To take every thought captive."

The enemy is the great complicator. He loves to send confusion, doubt, and hopelessness, which makes you think it must be hard, it must be difficult, it must have a very high price in order for me to get this. That's exactly what the devil wants you to think, because those thoughts lead to total destruction.

How effective are you in the marketplace against the kingdom of darkness with that kind of thought going through your head? You are not at all effective. Do not allow the enemy to rob you of your purpose, your inheritance, your destiny.

Before meeting Dani Johnson, I had spent close to $100,000 on personal growth seminars and workshops, only to find myself living from paycheck to paycheck, renting a room in someone else's home, dealing with bad relationships. Since training with Dani Johnson I have never had to interview for any positions I have held... employers recruited me! If you know someone who needs help with people skills, encouragement, or a new direction for their life, then they need to discover the Dani Johnson system now."

~ Dawn L.

FACING YOUR GIANTS

W E ARE GOING to look at 1 Samuel. When I rededicated my life to the Lord, and felt like I could do no good for God because of my profession, this book had a profound impact on me. I really thought that my profession was my profession, and if I was a really good Christian, then I would become a pastor or I would become some kind of a teacher. I had been leading people for 16 years, and here I am thinking I am no good for the church. I felt that I was lesser of a person in the church. I had felt that for years and years.

Let's again look at David. He sliced off heads and foreskins, and he was the apple of God's eye. Although he was a murderer and adulterer, he was the apple of God's eye. Kind of shatters the religious doctrine that says you better be perfect, doesn't it? He did not set you free for the sake of going into bondage trying to be perfect. That's not what it's about. They crucified the only perfect One.

So, David is 16 years old, and he gets anointed as king over Israel. There is still a current king in Israel named Saul, who is a wicked king. God then says, "I'm removing my spirit from Saul. Samuel, go anoint one of these eight sons over there in Bethlehem." So, he goes to Bethlehem to find a house with Jesse. He sees seven of the sons, and he says, "Oh, this eldest one. He must be the one that you want anointed king." I Samuel 16:7 says, "But the Lord says to Samuel, do not consider his appearance or his height, for I have rejected him.

The Lord does not look at the thing man looks at. Man looks at the outward appearance, but the Lord looks at the heart."

Why was David chosen over his brothers? He's the youngest, the baby of the family. Why was he chosen? He was chosen because of his heart and not because of his skill or ability. Not because he was the best and strongest. No, he was chosen because he had a heart after God.

Guess what David's very first job was, after he was anointed king over Israel, while there is still yet another king? He's anointed and then many years later he becomes king. Do you have any idea what happens to David after he's anointed king? He plays the harp. Saul hears about David's ability to play the harp. God sends a tormenting spirit to Saul because of his disobedience. One of Saul's bearers says, "Hey, listen. I know this kid in Bethlehem. He plays the harp, and I hear the spirits leave whenever he plays." Saul says, "I want him."

So, he calls for him. David comes. Sure enough, Saul's being tormented by an evil spirit. David begins to play the harp and the evil spirit leaves. So, every time Saul is tormented, David comes. He worships the Lord in the king's presence, and the demonic spirit leaves. So, his first job as king was to serve. That's your first job as a king in the marketplace, to serve.

We all know the story of David and Goliath. In 1 Samuel 17:4 Saul has been treated by worship from David, then there's a war against the Philistines, and it says, "A champion named Goliath, who was from Gath, came out of the Philistine camp. He was over nine feet tall. He had a bronze helmet on his head, and wore a coat of scale armor of bronze weighing 5,000 shekels; on his legs he wore bronze greaves and a bronze javelin was slung on his back. His spear shaft was like a weaver's rod and its iron point weighed 600 shekels. His shield bearer went ahead of him."

This is a giant man, who's extremely strong and well-armored. What happens here is that Goliath now stood and shouted to the ranks of Israel: "Why do you come out and line up for battle? Am I not a Philistine and are you not the servants of Saul? Choose a man and have him come down to me. If he is able to fight and kill me, we will become your subjects; but if I overcome him and kill him, you will become our subjects and serve us." (1 Samuel 17:8-9) It continues on verse 10: "Then the Philistines said, This day, I defy the ranks of Israel! Give me a man and let us fight each other. On hearing the Philistine's words, Saul and all the Israelites were dismayed and terrified."

In verse 26 David asked the man standing near him, "What will be done for the man who kills the Philistine and removes this disgrace from Israel? Who is this uncircumcised Philistine that he should defy the armies of the Living God? They repeated to him what they had been saying and told him, 'This is what will be done for the man who kills him.'" In verse 25 it says: "The king will give great wealth to the man who kills him. He will also give him his daughter in marriage and exempt his father's family from taxes in Israel."

Next it says, what David said was overheard and reported to Saul and Saul sent for him. David said to Saul, "Let no one lose heart on account of this Philistine. Your servant will go out and fight him." Saul replied, "Dude, calm down" That's Dani's version. "You're young, man. Cool your jets!" David said to Saul, "Your servant has been keeping his father's sheep."

When a lion or a bear came and carried off the sheep from the flock, I went after it, struck it and rescued the sheep from its mouth. When it turned on me, I seized it by its hair, struck it and killed it. Your servant has killed both lions and a bear. This uncircumcised Philistine will be like one of them, because he has defied the armies of the Living God, the Lord who delivered me from the paw of the lion and the paw of the bear, will deliver me from the hand of this Philistine."

Saul said to David, "Go, and the Lord be with you." Then Saul dressed David in his own tunic. Basically, Saul gave his armor to little David and he put it on him. David said, "I can't move." Can we take this off?"

In verse 40 it says "he took his staff in his hand, chose five smooth stones from the stream, put them in the pouch of his shepherd bag, and with his sling in his hand approached the Philistine. Meanwhile, the Philistine with his shield bearer in front of him kept coming closer to David. He looked David over and saw that he was only a boy, ruddy and handsome, and he despised him. He said to David, 'Am I a dog that you come at me with sticks?' And the Philistine cursed David by his God. 'Come here,' he said, 'and I will give your flesh to the birds of the air and the beasts of the field.'"

David said to the Philistine, "You come against me with the sword and spear and a javelin, but I come against you in the name of the Lord Almighty, the God of the armies Israel, whom you have defiled. This day, the Lord will hand you over to me and I will strike you down, and cut off your head. Today I will give the carcasses of the Philistine army to the birds of the air and the beasts of the earth, and the whole world will know that there is a God in Israel."

Are you getting it? Let me help you. Are you facing some giants right now? Where is your fight? It says that David absolutely went forward after him. Are you running from your giants? Do you have a giant debt? Do you have a giant fear? Are you facing a huge armored giant? How about a big, heavy, ugly giant with a big mouth?

David said to Goliath, "Come on, buddy, let's go at it. Put 'em up, let's go." Where's your fight? Ask yourself. Do your circumstances determine your faith, your strength and your forward moving action? If a hundred people tell you "no," does that determine, or does that have anything to do with your faith? Does it waiver your faith when you hear a hundred no's? Does it waiver your faith when you look at your desk? Does it waiver your faith when you look at your house?

You cannot allow your circumstances to determine your faith. You cannot allow your circumstances to determine your strength. You cannot allow your circumstance to determine your fight.

Do you want to become a king in the marketplace as a child of the Most High God? Well then, you must face your giants because that's what David had to do. David is exalted as the favored king in the entire Bible, next to Jesus Christ. Jesus Christ came from the line of David.

Do you realize that? God said, "I will establish your house forever," and He has. In order for you to be a king in the marketplace and used mightily by God, you have to face your giants. The giants of fear, debt, people who are against you. Face the giants of anxiety, fear and worry. Slay those suckers.

What rose up in David? The warrior is what rose up in David. The Holy Spirit rose up in him and said, "Fight the good fight of faith because I'll be with you." Do you see how big your giants are and how small you are? Or how big your God is? Do you see how powerful your giants are and how weak you are? Or do you see the power of the Spirit of the Living God that dwells within you is who 2,000 years ago slay every single one of those giants you are facing today? You have three choices - How strong they are and how weak you are, or how God's strength within you can overcome.

The Bible says that Jesus within you is the hope of glory. The Bible says that I can do all things through Christ who strengthens me. It doesn't say all things except being successful. It doesn't say all things except getting over my debt. It doesn't say all things except my cancer. It doesn't say all things except my boss. It doesn't say all things except my husband or my wife. No, it says all things are possible. All things—I can do all things through Christ who strengthens me. I don't care how big your giant is, Christ within you can overcome absolutely anything.

It says, "All things are possible for those who are in Christ Jesus." I'm a living testimony to that scripture. It's Him within me that strengthened me to do the things I did not know I could do. Why? He is a good God. And the devil's a bad devil and he's stupid. He's predictable.

Have you seen how your God has already defeated the powers of the giant? This is nothing for Him. It doesn't matter what it is you're facing, no matter how big it is, no matter how big the problem is, what a disaster it is. He's bigger. These things are nothing but a test of your faith. Will you trust Him? That's the question.

So the giant circumstances could be disease and sickness in your body. Giant circumstances could be lack of finances, your marriage, your teenagers, your job, or relationships with people. You have to look back and say, "Okay, what did David do?" Let me tell you what he did.

1) He attacked his giant without hesitation.

So, attack without hesitation. If the giant is finances, then you attack without hesitation. Do what it takes to learn to get out of debt and increase your skill set so you can increase your income. With the fervor that David had when he picked up those five stones and said, "Come on, buddy. I do not come at you with a javelin or a spear or sword I come at you with the Spirit of the Most High God." That's what he came at him with. There was no fear. Why? Because his eyes were centered upon the One who delivered him in the past from bears and lions. His eyes were not on his size or Goliath's size it was on the God of Israel who parted the Red Sea.

There was no fear. Why? Because let me tell you something. Fear enters when there is indecision and procrastination. That's when fear enters. He did not hesitate. He saw a giant defying the armies of the Most High God. "Buddy, you're going to die today." And he attacked. So you go and you attack, and you attack it big time, knowing that if He is for you, then who can be against you?

2) He fought with God's strength

I love what Ephesians 6:12 says. It says, "For our struggle is not against flesh and blood, but against the rulers, against the authorities, against the powers of this dark world, and against the spiritual forces of evil in the heavenly realms." Even though you're fighting with your spouse, it has nothing to do with your spouse. It says, "It's against the rulers and against the authorities, against the powers of this dark world, against the spiritual forces of evil." It's the evil forces working within the person you are fighting, in the Heavenly realms. Let's talk about weapons. David's weapon against Goliath was faith.

3) Seek

Seek means you've got to leave your house and go get busy. Faith, just words, means nothing, which is why the scriptures say that faith without works is dead. You have to prove your faith by getting off your butt and getting busy. If you are suffering from cancer, some kind of physical thing wrong with your body and just waiting to die, that is not faith. Faith says: "You know what? I don't care what happens, I am going to go where I have to go, I'm going to do whatever I have to do to have this body be restored. Whatever it is you got for me, I want it, I'll try anything." Faith isn't sitting around waiting for things to happen. The Bible then says, "When you come to the door,"- what are you supposed to do? "Knock."

I'm sure that when Christ walked the earth there were people who were sick and did not want to go to Him. Perhaps when they got there, they didn't ask, they didn't seek, and they didn't knock. Pathetic!

3) Trust

This is huge. This is enormous. Psalms 28:7 says, "My heart trusts in Him, and I am helped." David said that. Isn't' that amazing? Psalm 84:12 says, "Blessed is the man who trusts in You." Proverbs 28:25-26, says, "A greedy man stirs up dissension, but he who trusts in the Lord will prosper. He who trusts in himself is a fool, but he who walks in wisdom is kept safe."

Let's read this again: "A greedy man stirs up dissension, but he who trusts in the Lord will prosper." Not, he who trusts in Dani. Not he who trusts in your company. Not he who trusts in yourself. Not he who trusts in the government. Not he who trusts in the economy. Not he who trusts in your house. Not he who trusts in his spouse. Not he who trusts in his boss. No, it says, "But he who trusts in the Lord, will prosper. He who trusts in himself is a fool. But he who trusts, walks in wisdom, is kept safe." He is worthy of all of your trust.

At the beginning of this book, I asked you a few questions. Are you satisfied financially, physically, mentally, emotionally, socially, relationally?

My hope, my prayer, is that you now realize the skills and abilities, dormant with in you that are, waiting to come out. Skills and abilities that will increase satisfaction in every of your life. You have the ability to do your heart's desire that because God designed you for success.

He did not intend for your life to be mediocre. Please, don't live your life condemned by your own excuses. Don't wait for the right circumstances because that time will never come. Don't wait until it's too late. Take ACTION! Do something! The Spirit of the Living God is ready and willing to use you, are you ready?

God truly does have a plan for your life. You have been anointed, set apart, filled to overflowing with all the tools and gifts you need to accomplish that plan, and He that is in you is ABLE to complete it!

Now you have a choice…

You can put down this book and go on living a mundane, predictable, mediocre, fearful life…OR you can respond to what you have just read and learn to like David, like Jesus…Go after it! Attack…

You can believe you are who HE has clearly says you are. Believe that He is who He says He is. Then, in that confidence, you can move forward! Step out of the rut you have been living in… the rut you have been calling your life, and RISE UP!

I manage real estate agents and my job was to train them. When I started training with Dani and implementing her techniques, as well as the attitude and posture that she teaches, the success of the office uncreased. Within 6 weeks I was promoted and transferred to a larger, more productive office inside the company.

~ Andrea A

YOUR NEXT STEP

R EADING IS A good start, but if you want long lasting results, you must put these principles of Spirit Driven Success into action daily! My first suggestion is that you read this book from start to finish once a month for the next year. The little voice in your head might be saying, "Why do I need to read the book again and again?" Simple, repetition is the mother of skill. The more you absorb the principles of Spirit Driven Success, the faster you'll see results in your life as you become the person God designed you to be.

Over the years I have had the honor and privilege of equipping over 100,000 people for success through my live seminars, tele-classes, audios, videos, personal coaching and mentoring programs. Through these training programs thousands have developed the skills to enrich their lives far beyond what they thought was possible.

The marketplace pays for value and the way you increase your value to the market is by increasing your skill. This book is the beginning of a lifelong journey of a true relationship with God through Jesus Christ and His Holy Spirit AND through ongoing development of your skills so that you can bring VALUE to the marketplace and create impact for His Kingdom.

To help you increase your skill, I would like to give you a complimentary membership to one of our member's only training sites. Here you will have access to audio, video, television programs and special reports valued at over $10,000 that will help you advance in all areas of your life 24 hours a day 7 days a week.

As a member, you'll be equipped to develop your skill set so that you can compete head to head in the market place and succeed wildly for His glory. The training tools in our member's sites will help you become a better business owner, marketer, CEO or executive, employee, salesperson, manager or supervisor, mother or father, school teacher, community leader, pastor or minister. Whatever occupation, career or business you are involved in, you'll find the free training resources invaluable.

To get instant access to these member's only tools, simply visit www.DaniJohnson.com right now and subscribe to one of our member's only sites.

Also, take advantage of my SPECIAL FREE CD OFFER!! For a limited time we are offering a complimentary copy of "Conquering the Financial Kingdom." Inside this CD you will discover how to avoid the 7 traps that rob your prosperity, the 10 laws of wealth, how the fruits of your choices show up in your finances, how God rewards your spirit of excellence and a whole lot more.

So don't delay, head over to www.DaniJohnson.com right now and get yourself registered as a complimentary Rise To Success.com or Work At Home Profit Zone.com member.

God truly does have a plan for your life. You have been anointed, set apart, filled to overflowing with all the tools and gifts you need to accomplish that plan, and He that is in you is ABLE to complete it!

Now you have a choice...

You can put down this book and go on living a mundane, predictable, mediocre, fearful life... OR you can respond to what you have just read and learn to, like David, like Jesus... Go after it! Attack...

You can believe you are who HE has clearly said you are. Believe that He is who He says He is. Then, in that confidence, you can move forward! Step out of the rut you have been living in... the rut you have been calling your life, and RISE UP!

A SPECIAL NOTE FROM DANI

Has Spirit Driven Success impacted your life? Has it made a difference in how you see yourself, how you see God and how you see your part in building His Kingdom? Do you plan to use the principles revealed in Spirit Driven Success to enrich your life spiritually and financially? Do you plan to use these principles to get a promotion or a raise at work, to start a new business, or to take an existing business from failure or struggling to exponential growth and success? Will you use Spirit Driven Success to become debt free and wealthy so that you may be that light on a hill that the world will see so that your Father in Heaven may be glorified?

If so, will you help me help others? Will you help me share the message of Spirit Driven Success with the rest of the world? If Spirit Driven Success has impacted you, if it has changed your life and set you free, who do you know that you would like to share this gift with? I am asking for your help, there are millions of Christians and non-Christians alike who are in bondage like I was. This message changed my life, and has now changed the life of tens of thousands of others for His glory. I want to see it spread across the world, because I know what my life would be today had I not received and acted on the principle's in this book – I don't even want to think about it. Will you help me spread this message? I can't do it alone, but you can make a huge difference. Will you?

If so, please consider the following ideas:

1. Make a list of names, of people you want to bless with Spirit Driven Success. Who do you know that has influence (pastor, community leader, board member, CEO or executive)? Who do you know in your church, school, work place? Who do you know that is a business owner or marketer? Who do you know that is struggling to make ends meat and needs a promotion at their job? Who do you know who doesn't yet know their true purpose in life? Who do you know in your family who needs to experience healing emotionally, mentally and spiritually?

2. Make that list right now and;

a. Call them right now and tell them about Spirit Driven Success. Tell them how it's impacted you and share your story. Give them our website (www.DaniJohnson.com or www. SpiritDrivenSuccess.com) where they can get their very own copy shipped out to them within 24 hours.

b. Go to our website and order multiple copies of the book as a gift. You can have the book shipped directly to your friends, business associates or family members as a gift from you. You can get discounts of up to 70% for bulk orders.

c. Go to www.SpiritDrivenSuccess.com and use our refer-a-friend feature to send an email invitation to your contacts to visit our website and get more info about Spirit Driven Success. You can use this tool to import your entire address book or contact list to receive a message from you (sent from our servers) about Spirit Driven Success.

As a special thank you for helping us get the word out about Spirit Driven Success, there are some Missing Chapters and Audio Files to the book that I want to give you completely free! You'll get instant access to them by following the steps above.

Thank you and may God bless and prosper you greatly!

~ Dani Johnson

DANI JOHNSON WANTS TO HEAR FROM YOU!!

Tell Dani how Spirit Driven
Success has impacted your life.

Submit your audio testimonial (preferred)
It's easy! Just call: 800-609-9006 Ext. 2991
(International callers: 678-255-2174 x2991)

OR

Email Dani at feedback-sds@danijohnson.com

OR

Send a letter through the mail:

Call to Freedom International, LLC
Spirit Driven Success Feedback
3225 S. McLeod Drive, Suite 100
Las Vegas, NV 89121

FOR MORE INFORMATION

For more information about Dani Johnson products and events,
or to find out more about Dani Johnson, contact:

Call to Freedom International
3225 S. McLeod Drive
Suite 100
Las Vegas, NV 89121
(866) 590-5999
www.DaniJohnson.com

ABOUT DANI JOHNSON

Dani Johnson is an author, speaker, trainer and founder of Call to Freedom Int'l. She went from living out of her car with $2.03 to her name to earning her first million in two short years by the age of 23. Through her dynamic training seminars many of her clients have become debt free and have gone on to earn six and seven figure incomes.

Dani teaches and coaches with a passionate desire to see her clients become transformed in their spiritual, family, and professional lives. Her clients become warriors in the marketplace, demonstrating God's glory in places where the church cannot reach.

Dani's passion is helping people break through barriers that stop them from experiencing true freedom emotionally, mentally, spiritually, and financially.